# UP ON MADISON DOWN ON 75TH

ALSO BY JON F. RICE

*Life in the Shadows of American History*

*Tales of the Martin Clan*

*Black Revolutionaries on Chicago's West Side: A History of the
Illinois Black Panther Party*

Jon F. Rice

Historical Preservation Society Press

Chicago

With special thanks to all those who helped, particularly four or five
dedicated associates who wish to remain nameless.

# TABLE OF CONTENTS

*To educate man to be actional, preserving in all his relations*

*his respect for the basic values that constitute a human world,*

*is the prime task of him who, having taken that thought,*

*prepares to act.*

— FRANZ FANON
*Black Skin / White Masks*

# PREFACE

I became interested in the Black Panther Party through my first job at the state reformatory, then in Wilmington, Illinois (later in Peoria). The boys at the reformatory were my first experience with the rough crowd, the urban poor, in which I wasn't dodging them on the streets in fear of losing my wallet or a fight. I got to see how tough their lives were and how strong they were up against that life. They were 13 through 16 years old, living in dorms in which assaults and intimidation were daily problems, in which there was consistent bullying and manipulation for food, candy, and clothes. They were often kids with no families, who never got visits, who longed for some affection from parents but never admitted it. They very seldom wilted in public. I never saw a tear in class or a kid who didn't wholeheartedly reject sympathy. (Not that they didn't cry, but they did it privately.)

White kids and black, for the most part, segregated themselves there, and I taught against that. It was the late 1960s, and there were heavy racial tensions throughout the society. At our school, black teens were about 70% of the population, and they dominated. They leaned on the weaker white kids while the stronger whites held their own. In this atmosphere, I taught history and reading, coached the baseball team (and lived at the school). I also taught them that they were all in the same boat and ought to learn to stick together. The kids generally rejected that line, while around me, on the "outside," middle-class college kids talked about their animosities toward whitey. Seemingly, their poorer brothers at the school thought somewhat the same.

Then, suddenly, a new group appeared: poor youths my age (22) and younger, preaching black/white solidarity. They were from the rough crowd, but they were putting their courage into political aspirations. They

were the Black Panther Party. I was interested, and I began first by reading
what they wrote, then I began making trips to Chicago to listen to them,
and finally, confronted by Chicago's attempts to annihilate them, I
was selling papers for them. Not that we agreed on anything but black/
white unity, yet I was angered that they were being so blatantly assaulted,
particularly after making that move to transcend racism. I was moved by
their courage. I got to know some of them and found that I liked many
of them. From that experience comes this attempt to document what they
did in Chicago, good and bad.

# INTRODUCTION

More than the South Side ghetto, Chicago's West Side was in the 1950s a 15- to 20-year-old refugee center, growing daily, something like the West Bank for Palestinians. Black people were coming north from Mississippi, hundreds of them daily. Chicago's second great black migration was on. They were being pushed off the land and their cultural base for three hundred years—the South—and put on the closest vehicle running north—the Illinois Central train. They came to a place where they found steady jobs only rarely. They, a productive rural people, put up camp in the big cold city by the lake, becoming a far less productive rural people controlled by an urban police force, like, say, the Italians of the 1890s.

The West Side's appearance as an old city was an illusion made by the old, crowded buildings. The people were alive and unified behind their Southern culture. It was a culture based on the extended family. Families were most important for West Siders; grandparents, aunts, uncles, cousins defined who you were. They hung together, conscious of their common oppressor, racist whites. If you could melt down in a few words what the family taught, what grandma, Aunt Rose, Uncle Will taught, the melted down lump would read in big letters, "Go to school and get educated (like we didn't have a chance to do down South) and don't take no stuff from these white folks, nor anyone else!"

The immediate oppressors for West Side black kids in the 1950s were the white clubs from Cicero, Illinois, and from west of Kostner Avenue, which was still white, who raided the black community. To escape serious injury from these clubs, it was wise to know how to run. In desperation, the police might be called out, but if they were white, and most were, they'd be apathetic—or side with the white boys and send the victim to the Audie Home. So, in response, black kids formed their own clubs, a phenomenon the media called gangs.

These youthful clubs took mystic, romantic names: the Egyptian Cobras, the Princes, the Clovers, the Apaches, the Navajoes. They were not, at first, into either crime or turf or into political control; they socialized and fought the white boys. They halted the civilian attacks on their community.

The West Side ghetto was materially poor, as was the South Side ghetto, but South Side poverty was noticeably different. There, poverty was perhaps more desperate, out of touch with Southern black roots. It was urbanized poverty, quiet poverty centered on the nuclear family; individualism had become the norm. There was a minority of black people there that had carved "success," financial success. The South Side had this class division that often ran right through families. Poorer relatives were often known to move to the West Side to get back to that "down home" feeling. Trouble was, there just wasn't enough success to share. So, the successful end of the South Side ghetto got a piece of the action, received better services, and often got police protection rather than police control. Black police who patrolled Grand Crossing or Chatham often lived there, and more often than not, those who patrolled Lawndale lived in Chatham or Grand Crossing too. Reflecting their community, South Side gangs were small. They fought each other over turf and harassed the successful's kids, as the growing black population spilled into new areas. Sometimes the West Side Cobras came south and ran them all around.

The political analogy that portrays the West Side as a colony ruled by whites and the South Side as neo-colonial, ruled by "our" blacks was accurate, but it was more than that. Some West Siders had financial success too, had money, but to them, success was a home in Alabama. They'd suffer here because they felt this wasn't necessarily home—yet.

The communities of the South and West Sides were changing. In the fifties, with fewer people employed by whites and more self-employed, with more hustlers like the rag man, the watermelon man, the doughnut man, the junk man, who drove rickety wagons through the streets, pulled by ancient horses, that community survived on community spirit. In those days, teachers, doctors, rag men, pimps, whores, all lived on the same streets. From 61st to 43rd, from Western to Pulaski, the pattern was integrated. Racial segregation was so strict that professionals couldn't get financing from white banks to buy homes; either you paid cash or did without. But in the late fifties, homeowning communities opened up to black Chicago as banks reversed their policies. The economic segregation of the expanding ghetto was increased by the rise of the super projects built specifically for the poor, Robert Taylor, the Henry Horner Homes, Cabrini-Green. Having escaped their poorer brothers, middle-class families could be discriminating. Yet, having escaped the poor ghetto by moving to Chatham or Maywood, the middle class, like the poor, found themselves just as fiercely segregated and discriminated against by their white neighbors and by city services. And by the 1960s, with the rise of activity in civil rights, they were less willing to take it.

July 10, 1965, was more than hot. Soldier's Field felt like a giant micro-oven dropped in a steam bath. It was over 100 degrees, so hot someone was fanning gospel singer Mahalia Jackson to keep her from fainting, so hot that the Andrew McPherson Quartet found their instruments almost too hot to hold.

The Quartet was playing "John Brown's Body" when suddenly fifty or more teenagers burst onto the playing field of the stadium, with a large, bright red flag. They were shouting something. Probably it was "Mighty Blackstone," for those were the Blackstone Rangers. They interrupted the Quartet, stopped Dr. Martin Luther King from coming out, and upset all the "muckety-mucks," as they circled the field on the run. Couldn't anyone stop them—stop these "toughs" from Woodlawn? Disc Jockey Herb Kent tried, but they ignored him; he didn't speak their language, he was an "Ivy Leaguer." They were "Gouster." Dick Gregory tried too, and they understood him, but this was their thing now—if he'd just be cool for a while. Meanwhile, the crowd got angry. "Call the police!" someone yelled, and everyone cheered the idea. The crowd thought the police were on their side. The police never came, and the club or "gang" raced into the upper-east side of the stadium and let the rally continue. It was Chicago's civil rights movement at its peak.

The turmoil of the early sixties was over segregation in public places, over job discrimination, and the denial of voting rights. These were the goals fought for ever since Jim Crow took the South by storm in the 1880s, fought for by Afro-American war veterans who'd fought in two World Wars for democracy only to come home to its denial for them in America. The push had never ceased and was coming to shove, but it was still optimistic of having a role in the system and supportive of

American capitalism. It was law-abiding here, though it sanctioned civil disobedience against laws it considered unjust. There was its potentially explosive sore spot with a city police department that tended to be racist. Generally speaking, they had no sympathy with that view and tended to see disorder, whether caused by demonstrators or gangsters, as criminal. The rally, by virtue of its focus, was potentially criminal. The people were, to many police, troublemakers looking for a way to cause trouble. The police didn't see the difference between them and gang-bangers, although they were trying to distance themselves from the rougher crowd. There was a transformation in the wind, pushed by just such attitudes as the police held. It was a distant cry in the wind whispering, "All power to the people, I'm high off the people, people love!"

The crowd of 40 to 50 thousand left Soldier's Field and marched to City Hall, waving at the television cameras. The Chicago media had been friendly to the movement down South, but now, well, they'd brought the movement North, and that would be different.

Thomas Greene

# Chapter 1

# THE CHICAGO FREEDOM MOVEMENT

**Civil Disorder in Chicago.** People from Chicago had gone South to join the Movement. It was the Chicago-based Congress of Racial Equality (CORE) that originated the "Freedom Bus" rides. Those courageous riders who forced integration on Greyhound buses by daring to ride through violent white mobs included Chicagoans, black and white. Even before that, it was black Chicagoans who supported evicted sharecroppers in Tennessee in 1959—evicted for daring to vote. Early supporters of the Movement included Bernita Howell, Gus Savage, Bob Lucas, Bennett Johnson, and Charles Reddick. It was Chicago CORE that put up picket lines around Chicago Woolworth stores so that Greensboro's movement would have Northern support.

The first battles in Chicago were over desegregated restaurants and other private businesses open to the public, like the White City roller rink in the late forties. But as the Movement heated up down South in the 1950s, that too brought increased activity in the North. The Movement hit Chicago in the early sixties, and the issue was overcrowded ghetto schools. In 1963, for example, Hirsch High School, on the South Side, built to hold 1,800 students, held 2,316.[1] It was typical of black high schools. There wasn't anywhere for black Chicagoans to move. Schools were so overcrowded that the Superintendent of Schools, Benjamin Willis, decided the solution was to set up trailers in ghetto school parking lots as extra classrooms. It was cheaper than building additions, easier than allowing black students to transfer, and, of course, beat unsegregated housing all to hell.

In June 1963, CORE, now under the leadership of World War II veteran Bob Lucas, began a sit-in at the Board of Education to demand a meeting on the desegregation of Chicago. Nine members of CORE simultaneously went on a hunger strike. After an entire month of sitting in and being ignored, they got a response—the Chicago police moved them out. CORE was determined, however, and come August, the issue was still alive. They'd gotten the support of popular comedian Dick Gregory, and they demanded the resignation of the establishment's defender of the status quo, Superintendent Ben Willis. However, the Chicago Board of Education continued on as if the protestors didn't exist. Up went the twenty-five mobile classrooms at the overcrowded schools. Like Bull Connor in the South, Chicago's Board of Education increased hostilities through its arrogance. The protestors called the trailers "Willis wagons," and at this point, the High School Friends of SNCC, led by Lawrence Landry, made its presence felt. Landry had created a student movement, evolving from a tutoring program, the Student Woodlawn Project. It expanded into several schools and became the student end of the newly created Coordinating Council of Community Organizations, some thirty community groups.

High School Friends of SNCC led 225,000 students[2] on a one-day boycott on Chicago schools on October 17, 1963. Right under his nose, Mayor Daley and the Democratic Party were confronted with a youth movement.

The Democratic Party went to work. Black leaders in the Party were put in opposition to the movement people. Black alderman Kenneth Campbell, Claude Holman, and Congressman William Dawson led the attack on their electorate. The organization they formed to stop the movement went under the misleading names of The Assembly to End Prejudice, Injustice and Poverty.[3] But the end of any of these three (prejudice, poverty, or injustice) would have put them in trouble; it would have eroded the very ghetto upon which their power stood. So those who screamed at these attempts to "unghetto" the ghetto were the black elected leaders of that ghetto. Black leaders found profit in segregation—in Chicago's tradition. In 1920, Oscar DePriest, the city's first black Congressman, made a bundle buying an apartment of whites and renting it to blacks—at the inflated rate for black renters. DePriest was also part of a blockbusting scheme that worked to expand the area where overcrowded blacks could live. They used white-looking blacks to do much of the opening up of blocks. But while DePriest made a profit, he also performed a service. Finessing the system, they call it. Black people did not mind him making a profit in the misery of ghetto Chicago in the 1920s; there wasn't much hope anyone else would find much better.

But this was the 1960s. Determination and optimism were in the air. Finding a profit in the midst of hopeless racial oppression was okay, but when the freedom train comes, trying to derail it so you can continue is traitorous. It was time to drop the traditions of second-class citizenship. Jubilee had come, and the black cynics in the Democratic Party were, from the activist viewpoint, one with the enemy.

The Coordinating Council of Community Organizations went on with plans for a second boycott despite the efforts of "their" aldermen. Mayor Daley suggested his boys pressure the parents to stop it. Daley got support from the local AME Church and Baptist leader Rev. Joseph H. Jackson and his ministers, some 400 in Chicago. They all urged parents to break the student boycott. Nevertheless, on February 25, 1964, some 172,350 students stayed away from school, by the Board of Education's own count! In Alderman Campbell's own 20th ward, schools were 90 percent empty.[4]

Here was indication that this movement had some power; it could resist Daley's best shot. Now it was the Democratic Machine versus CCCO. Already, the news media seemed to be slipping over into the Daley camp, as they "found" the cause of rising violence in the schools to be the activists (not those who ignored the activists and tried to move on like they weren't there).

This second boycott was followed by counter-marches by white parents who feared the effects of a victory for the activists, and by a court injunction against boycotts. The court injunction was followed by another boycott. Then, civil rights "militants" were sitting down in the expressways at rush hour. Arrests followed escalating protests, and the arrests became a little rougher, finally breaking out into fights with the police, whose patience had generally reached the edge. Marchers now picketed Daley's Bridgeport home and Benjamin Willis's home.[5] By late 1965, the movement hadn't died, Dick Gregory was in jail, and Daley was charging communists led the movement.[6] No resolution was in sight, and so the issue slipped from school desegregation to segregation in housing, which, of course, made for segregated schools. Lawrence Landry and Al Raby, leaders of CCCO, sought and got the attention of the Southern Christian Leadership Conference (SCLC), which decided that Chicago, as the epitome of urban segregation, could be a test case for SCLC nonviolent tactics in an urban setting. And so King moved on Daley's town, CCCO took on housing, and all hell was about to break loose. Caught up in it all were Bob Brown, Fred Hampton, Bobby Rush, and perhaps one-fifth of teenage black Chicago.

Bob Lucas, a quiet, unassuming man, had been active in the civil rights movement for several years. An unconventional thinker, he'd been part of a movement that had run a black candidate, Bennett Johnson, in a white ward to expose the racism in the Democratic Party. That was in the 1950s, and Johnson had been shot at for his effort, which the media ignored. But Lucas knew that vulnerability of the Democrats was still there. The Party was a coalition of blacks and white ethnics, and open housing marches could expose the hypocrisy of that alliance and tear it apart. It could be a bargaining tool for forcing the Democrats to cooperate. They refuse? Okay, let's march on Bridgeport, turn subtle racism out into the open, and split the coalition. Why not? It would not hurt black people any more than they were already being hurt, and it might wake people up to the need for an alternative.

The one ingredient marches required was the courage to march on the white communities bordering the ghetto because everyone in the know knew what would happen once these communities were marched on. As Bob Lucas stated it, he had risked his life for democracy in Germany in 1942, so why not risk it here for some democracy at home?

To the less sophisticated younger marchers, open housing marches were a continuation of the non-violent movement in the South. They regarded the marches as demonstrations against the evil of racism. They would hopefully overcome racism with love. But Bob Lucas, Gus Savage, Bennett Johnson, and Richard Daley knew the urban reality, and the rest would soon learn. Idealism based on non-violence could be stopped with violence.

Local white ethnics had fought for years to preserve what their sweat had created—a community relatively free from crime and overcrowding and free of black people, who, in their minds, brought crime and overcrowding wherever they came. Confronted with the actual, physical reality of their fearful fantasies, that is, real black people marching on their enclaves, they attacked with a frenzy, particularly in the march through Marquette Park on Chicago's South Side. Englewood and Marquette Park had been at war for the last two decades, and this is where open, organized hostilities began.

Two hundred open-housing idealists had assembled, young, old, black, white, priests and nuns, ministers, and Blackstone Rangers (serving as parade marshals). Led by Dr. King, Al Raby, and Jesse Jack- son, to name a few, they marched under attack from shouting crowds, bottles, and bricks, an attack that intensified as they went along. The crowd was just warming up. Discovering the marchers' cars parked around the Marquette Park Lagoon, they turned them over, split open the gas tanks, and tossed in lighted matches. Amidst the dull booms of exploding gas tanks, heard blocks away, the marchers found their police protection suddenly melting away, and then the full, unhindered fury of the mob was on them. A special rage seemingly was reserved for the white marchers, particularly the nuns. The crowd felt most threatened by these symbols of "their" society being against them. The marchers were forced to use their wits to get back to Englewood alive.

That Woodlawn (the South Side east of Cottage Grove Blvd.) club known as the "Stones" soon became their heroes, leaping into the air to catch thrown rocks, bottles, and bricks. Meanwhile, local leader "Ma" Houston prayed loudly and not ineffectively, "Oh Lord, you see that boy in the plaid shirt with the brick? Make him put that brick down, Lord! You see that man with the cherry bomb? Tell him not to throw it, Lord...!"[7]

Once back in Englewood, the marchers, who'd protected each other, had picked up their wounded (knocked unconscious by bricks), reassembled on 71st Street to treat their injuries. The floor of the New Friendship Baptist Church ran red with blood.[8] The tough, segregated suburb of Cicero, supposedly dominated by the Mafia, which bordered the ghetto of Lawndale, would be next.

Back on the Southeast Side, in Kenwood, black alderman Claude Holman was still trying to disrupt the movement. He had his boys, including 300-pound "Tiny" Wilson, hanging around places where rallies were held, taking names of people they knew. People began to avoid the rallies, believing that, at the very least, they'd lose a place to stay or a job.

Before the Cicero march came off, Dr. King and Mayor Daley reached what was called a summit agreement, an open-housing agreement—without Bob Lucas. Daley knew who to deal with alright, for this agreement, lacking any means of enforcement, was nothing less than a defeat for the movement. King called off the marches, packed up, and moved on, and the marchers got nothing but vague promises. Young people were more than a little aroused; they were angry.

Now, there was a rumor that black folks didn't have the nerve to march into Cicero, that Daley had called their bluff, and they had backed off. Lucas, who immediately recognized the summit agreement for the failure it was, got CORE to sponsor a march on Cicero.

There were people in Chicago in 1966 who would march to hell and back if it meant another step toward freedom from racial discrimination. Two hundred-ninety-three CORE marchers walked into Cicero, Illinois, on September 7, 1966, just weeks after black Jerome Huey had been beaten to death for job hunting in that same suburb. CORE'S message was that the summit agreement ended nothing and that Cicero needed to know Afro-Americans were not intimidated.

Five blocks into Cicero, the fury of the white mob not only stopped the marchers but turned back the Illinois National Guard. Non-violence could be stopped. The Chicago Freedom Movement died that day, while, generally speaking, the enthusiasm of young Afro-Americans was on the rise. Non-violence had never been their thing. Dr. King was gone, segregated public places were disappearing in the South, but the ghetto was still overcrowded, poorly serviced, unhealthy, and powerless. Across the nation, 1967 was a turning point for the urban centers. Detroit and Newark went up in flames. The government sent in the National Guard, but they could not stop it. Then they sent in tanks and combat troops. In Chicago, the Nazi Party marched through the South Side, and the police department that couldn't protect the civil rights marchers was very efficient at protecting the Nazis. They were armed and everywhere, on rooftops, on elevated platforms, aggressive and ready to shoot or crack heads, or so it appeared. Here was an education that was bound to make black people angry. And for the more studious, the writings of Malcolm X were receiving the attention they'd missed when he was alive. As army trucks rolled through both Lawndale and the South Side, though the South Side had been quiet, and Lawndale had gone up in flames the day that King was killed, people were ready for a new response to racial oppression, one that took in the education they had just received.

Now that he was safely dead, Dr. King became the media's hero. But he never communicated well in Chicago, among its youth, anyway. Malcolm made more sense, was more understandable. His way was common sense applied to a political goal, liberation. Use any tactics that work, he said. Here's an example of his views concerning nonviolence. It was fine when it worked, but when it does not, try something else, and don't be non-violent without cause, protect yourself:

> ...in Germany, they're violent in the South Pacific, they're
> violent in Cuba, they're violent wherever they go. But when
> it comes time for you and me to protect ourselves against
> lynchings, they tell us to be nonviolent.

> That's a shame. Because we get tricked into being nonviolent,
> and when somebody stands up and talks like I just did, they
> say, 'Why, he's advocating violence.' Isn't that what they
> say? Everytime you pick up your newspaper, you see where
> one of these things has written into it that I am advocating
> violence. I have never advocated any violence. I have only said
> that black people who are the victims of organized violence
> perpetuated upon us by the Klan, the Citizens Councils, and
> many other forms, should defend ourselves. And when I say
> we should defend ourselves against the violence of others,
> they use their press skillfully to make the world think that I
> am calling for violence, period. I wouldn't call on anyone to
> be violent without cause. But I think the black man in this
> country, above and beyond people all over the world, will be
> more justified when he stands up and starts to protect himself,
> no matter how many necks he has to break, and heads he has
> to crack....

> Now, for saying something like that, the press calls us racist
> and people who are 'violent in reverse.' This is how they psych
> you. They make you think that if you try to stop the Klan
> from lynching you, you're practicing violence in reverse. Pick
> up on this, I hear a lot of you parrot what the man says. You
> say, '"I don't want to be a Ku Klux Klan in reverse.' Well if a
> criminal comes around your house with his gun, brother, just
> because he's got a gun and he's robbing your house, and he's
> a robber, it doesn't make you a robber because you grab your
> gun and run him out. NO, the man is using some tricky logic
> on you. I say it is time for black people to put together the
> type of action, the unity that is necessary to pull the sheet off

them, so they won't be frightening black people any longer. That's all. And when we say this, the press calls us 'racists in reverse.' 'Don't struggle except within the ground rules that the people you're struggling against have laid down.' Why, this is insane, but it shows how they can do it. With skillful manipulating of the press they're able to make the victim look like the criminal and the criminal look like the victim.[9]

The press did, in fact, deliberately misinterpret Malcolm. Here's an example from *U.S. News and World Report*, entitled "His Theme Is Now Violence."

> Brother Malcolm's split with the sect has many Negro leaders worried. He commands a large following in Harlem. In racially troubled cities, his new line of preaching could stir up serious trouble for the whole civil rights movement.

> How much trouble, time will tell. The fact is that, for the first time, a Negro leader is openly trying to woo his race away from nonviolence. He is telling all who will listen: 'The Negro is justified to take any steps at all to achieve his equality...There can be no revolution without bloodshed.'[10]

Malcolm X, who by 1964 had changed his name to El Hajj Malik El-Shabazz, reached through the distortions of the news media and touched Afro-Americans with a message. He reached the street brothers first because not only did he speak their language, but because they were already aware of how the news media distorted their reality. He set people to thinking something different than how can I escape the ghetto; rather, how can the ghetto become an independent community? People were becoming aware that the strength they had had to develop to survive in the ghetto was the same strength that makes art, music, and language out of frustration. Perhaps the same strength could make liberation out of the ghetto colony.

In Chicago, in April 1968, a black political convention was held at Phil Cohran's Afro-Arts Theatre at 39th and Drexel, attracting people from across the country. Phil, a former member of the semi-nationalist but formally non-political Nation of Islam, had gone political, as had many "Black Muslims." Elijah Muhammad taught that God would personally save the "so-called Negro." But he also taught that Afro-Americans were like a man in the dark eating a maggot-filled sandwich (the American system). Once the light is turned on, the man puts the sandwich down, and nothing will make him pick it back up. Likewise, once black people got enlightened, they would put America down and return to their original "Asiatic" culture. Phil was about precisely that enlightenment.

The convention drew activists. It drew Stokely Carmichael and Ron Karenga, it drew a representative from the new Black Panther Party in Oakland, California, members of the Republic of New Africa, and of the Black Liberation Alliance. One fiery speaker stood out at that convention; he electrified the crowd. He was 19-year-old Fred Hampton of Maywood. He called for armed resistance to violent racist oppression. It was the spirit of the times, and Fred articulated it so well.[11]

**Maywood, 1966-67.** Fred Hampton's brief life began on August 30th, 1948. Seventeen years later, his career as an Afro-American leader emerged in Maywood, Illinois. Maywood was a troubled town where racial tensions, previously low-key, were growing. In the summer of 1966, for example, Mrs. Helen Mascio committed suicide, probably over the harassment she had received from city officials from selling her house in an all-white section of town to a black family. That's what the suicide letter said, at least.[12] Her death seemed to move people like few other things had, and brought concerted action from the Maywood Lutheran Human Relations Council to seek to bridge the gap between the races. They began to do some rather revolutionary things, like seek out Afro-American leaders to come and talk to white folks about racism in Maywood. As Joan Elbert recalls, the most articulate of these leaders was young Fred Hampton, president of the Youth Council of the Maywood NAACP. Fred forced young white folks to come to grips with their own attitudes of superiority, attacking the racism in their own personal outlook rather than what other people were doing. And in the following summer, when Maywood exploded in racial fights, it was this same Fred Hampton who cooled off a crowd of about 300 black teenagers and then led them on a peaceful march on City Hall. Fred was a natural leader, quick-thinking, unafraid, and confident. He was a voracious reader of history and politics and equally enthusiastic about listening to recorded speeches of Malcolm X, Dick Gregory, and Dr. King. To all who knew him, it was clear he was a future leader. And that year, 1967, his name appeared in the files of the FBI as someone to be watched (and harassed?).

Not long after the march on City Hall, Fred was arrested by the Maywood police. He was identified, after some illegal coaching, it seems, as the leader of a criminal gang that had robbed an ice cream truck and distributed all the ice cream. Fred, never known as a troublemaker, well-known as a good kid, was arrested and charged.

Being falsely arrested by those who supposedly uphold the system is a guaranteed way to make more trouble in the calmest of times. But in 1967, at the time Cicero mobs were beating Jerome Huey to death and getting away with it, when the Nazis were marching through black Chicago with excellent protection from the police, with troops in the streets and strife in the wind, it's a very dumb move—or a very arrogant one. The get-high crowd was acting irresponsibly; the brick throwers were free, but responsible Fred was being fingerprinted. Evidently, they were more serious about side-tracking the Movement than about the law. And Fred, like many Afro-Americans, was being victimized. The tumult of the times had brought subtle racism out of the closet. Seemingly, they were intent on stopping black Americans without regard to the justice of the individual situations. But Fred was preparing himself to help his people respond to this indiscriminate oppression. He would turn the oppressor's thinking on its head. You oppress us indiscriminately; we unify indiscriminately.

In May of 1968, Fred met a black activist and lecturer from Los Angeles, Lennie Eggleston. Watts had just recently exploded in the biggest riot yet, and so everyone was looking for L.A. speakers at the time. Fred had worked with white people, but he was, at this point, a black nationalist; his primary interest was black liberation, and the wisdom of folk experience, if not his own experiences, taught him that some of his most stubborn enemies were those poor whites who should have been allies. So Fred argued with Eggleston's assertion that poor whites and the working class were the natural allies of the struggle. The particulars of the argument have been lost or forgotten, but part of Eggleston's line was that black was being pitted against white, and vice versa, by the ruling class and their media. The issue of race oppression is a cover for class oppression.[13] And they, the poor, are encouraged to take their frustrations out on each other. Eggleston's assertion that we were not to give in to the way poor whites felt, that we were to think past it and ally with them, not let their thoughts define us but let our thoughts move them. It was just the kind of idea that appealed to Fred's creative mind; he was always looking for a new way of looking at an old problem, and he had the proselytizing fervor; that bit about defining your own reality must have caught his imagination. He was changing from a black nationalist to a socialist for all the people.

To Fred, who had seen the Chicago Freedom Movement only begin to move poor blacks in over four years of struggle, perhaps the class analysis also explained their limited success and the cynicism of the poor. They were aroused and then deserted, used, then left. Just as people were beginning to see the point, the marches were called off, and for what? What did they get when King and Daley shook hands? The leaders were always preaching, but did they take time to listen? Did they allow the masses to lead them? It's an old story; the poor in the Afro-American ghetto are deservedly suspicious of anyone supposedly interested in them.

Fred Hampton was ready to transcend the unacknowledged class bias in the movement, to transcend the traditional civil rights approach based on the interests of the let-us-into-the-status-quo crowd, even ready to transcend race, broadening the movement toward a unity-based, inclusive ideology. Fred had Dr. King's infectious optimism about the human spirit, but his appeal was to the gut rather than to America's soul. For Fred was finished with sit-ins, kneel-ins, pray-ins and requests, however courageously made. The message in the wind was, "Look out motherfucker, we taking what's ours!"

Fred was walking into a situation recklessly, studying, reading about Western society, what made it tick, how it responded, figuring out what would work. He knew he was being reckless about his own life. He knew there were racists ready to kill him, but he knew if he were on target, it wouldn't be ignorant racists who wanted him dead; it would be, from his new perspective, their mutual enemy—the man, the establishment.

# Chapter 2

# BIRTH OF THE PANTHER PARTY

The Black Panther Party was the spiritual heir of Malcolm X, according to its founders, and so if you read what Malcolm was saying, you get an idea of its spirit. Here's an example:

> Look at yourselves. Some of you are teenagers, students. How do you think I feel—and I belong to a generation ahead of you—how do you think I feel to have to tell you, 'We, my generation, sat around like a knot on a wall while the whole world was fighting for its human rights—and you've got to be born into a society where you still have that same fight? What we do, who preceded you? I'll tell you what we did: Nothing. And don't you make the same mistakes we made...

> You get freedom by letting your enemy know that you'll do anything to get your freedom; then you'll get it. When you get that kind of attitude, they'll label you as a 'crazy Negro,' or they'll call you a 'crazy nigger'—they don't say Negro. Or they'll call you an extremist, or a subversive, or seditious, or a red, or a racial. But when you stay radical long enough and get enough people to be like you, you'll get your freedom.

> So don't you run around here trying to make friends with somebody who's depriving you of your rights. They're not your friends, no, they're your enemies. Treat them like that and fight them, and you'll get your freedom and after you get your freedom, your enemy will respect you. And we'll respect you.

And I say that with no hate. I don't have hate in me. I have no hate at all. I don't have any hate, I've got some sense. I'm not going to let somebody who hates me tell me to love him. I'm not that way out. And you, as young as you are, and because you start thinking, you're not going to do it either. The only time you're going to get in that bag is if somebody puts you there. Somebody else, who doesn't have your welfare at heart...

— Malcolm X, "To Mississippi Youth," 1964

The Panther Party was born with that attitude, critical of former generations, and determined to be free at whatever cost, in two very different places with some very different political thrusts. First, there was a Black Panther Party formed by SNCC, evolving out of their voter registration drive in Lowndes County, Alabama.

In 1965, Lowndes County, population 15,000, was 80 percent black, with no registered black voters. There were 1,900 eligible white voters, of whom 2,500, or 130 percent, were registered. When SNCC, led by Stokely Carmichael, moved to help blacks register, their strongest opposition came from the Democratic Party. "Democratic" resistance to black voting rights included illegal eviction of farmers, intimidation, and violence. And so the people of Lowndes County bravely formed a brand new, independent political party, the Lowndes County Freedom Organization (LCFO). Their rationale reflected the spirit of the times nationwide. To quote from one of their founders:

We decided to stop begging. We've decided to stop asking for integration. Once we control the courthouse, once we control the board of education, we can build our school system where our boys and girls can get an education in Lowndes County. There are 89 prominent families in this country who own 90 percent of the land. These people will be taxed. And we will collect these taxes. And if they don't pay them, we'll take their property and sell it...

We aren't asking any longer for protection...and we won't need it [we'll protect ourselves]."

As a bona fide political party, they were legally required in Alabama to take an animal symbol. They chose the Panther; he was black and, by nature, peaceful unless provoked. Then he turned vicious on his attackers. They soon became known, by their symbol, as the Black Panther Party. They also were successful in Alabama in making independent politics viable, despite the efforts of Dr. Martin Luther King and SCLC to incorporate blacks in Alabama into the Democratic Party and ignore the Panther Party. Carmichael set forth the new agenda, an agenda they now planned to carry into neighboring Southern states and Northern cities.

> The Lowndes County Freedom Organization is not nonviolent. Nonviolence is irrelevant. What King has working for him is moral force, but we are building a force to take power. We are not a protest movement. We're out to take power legally, but if we're stopped by the government from doing it legally, we're going to take it the way everyone else took it, including the way Americans took it in the American Revolution. And we've seen the way the federal government protects us or rather doesn't protect us. If one of our candidates get touched, we're going to take care of the murderers ourselves.

Quickly mislabelled as anti-white, the Party responded by saying they must split with the "traitorous" Democratic Party, but they were not rejecting coalitions between blacks and whites; they simply would not accept such alliances on the grounds that they subordinate their needs to others.

This was in May 1966. Later that summer, 2,550 miles away, a couple of black young men at Merritt College in Oakland, California, were also forming a Black Panther Party—for self-defense from the police! Its original goal was to protect citizens from police abuses. They armed themselves and patrolled the police patrolling Oakland, curbing police brutality by their presence. They then drafted a 10-point political program for black liberation nationwide. They thought of themselves as a local group expressing a national mood, and they couldn't have been more accurate.

On May 2nd, 1967, this second group, led by Huey P. Newton and Bobby Seale, sent 23 armed "lobbyists" into the California legislature, ostensibly to protest gun control, and suddenly got coast-to-coast headlines. The genuinely revolutionary heroism of independent black politics in rural, KKK-ridden Alabama had been ignored by the national press, but the theatrical dramatics of California were "good stuff." Stokely, head of SNCC, was drawn by the press attention to move to Oakland and align his group with theirs. And so, as Eldridge Cleaver put it, the activists from the Bible belt joined the brothers from the gun belt.

In Chicago, the Friends of SNCC laid the groundwork for a Panther Party Chapter there to give Stokely's group a base in what was becoming a big-city phenomenon. SNCC recruited at Wilson Junior College (Kennedy-King) and at Crane (Malcolm X College). They got several students involved, including returning veterans from Vietnam, tough young men, ex-paratroopers, Marines, as well as students who'd never been away from home. They incorporated an entire self-defense group, then known as the Mau-Mau, and together, they renamed themselves the Illinois Black Panther Party.

They were the only group on the South Side, but in Chicago, they were not alone. The West Side was starting two Panther Parties. One was run by activist Russ Meeks, and another started by a former member of Fats Crawford's Deacons for Defense and Justice. The Deacons were members of the National Rifle Association and provided guards for activists who visited Chicago, such as Dr. King, Carmichael, Rap Brown. They also monitored white racist groups and raised funds for voter registration drives in the South. This second West Side group had two good leaders and was organizing in the area around Madison and Western, a neighborhood where Southern ways were strong and the feelings warm, though poverty was rampant. They were Southerners who had organized before to stop the various white ethnic gangs from running over them. Mile Square, as the neighborhood was called, soon had a strong Panther Party with people in charge who knew Bobby Seale and Elderidge Cleaver.

In August, they got Seale and Cleaver's promise to speak at a rally they planned at the Senate Theatre at Madison and Kedzie. They leafletted and talked about the rally and got a good crowd, but neither Seale nor Cleaver was able to come. Somehow, word of the rally did reach the SNCC crowd, however. Perhaps someone came to them with a leaflet saying, "Look here, I thought you guys were the Panthers." So, among those who attended the rally were twenty or so ex-SNCC members wearing black tams and calling themselves the Black Panthers. They were led by a former member of CORE, Robert Alfonso Brown, who at age 19 was already on the FBI list of "extremely militant" somebodies. This particular somebody was somebody they felt they needed "to remove from the scene, through some form of legal *or* police action [emphasis added]." An FBI memo also stated that one of the SNCC people whom he led was an informant of theirs.*

> *From SAC, Chgo (157-2209) Subj: Counterintelligence
> BNHG [Black Nationalist Hate Groups], 11/7/68 "SNCC...
> is virtually defunct...Chgo div Informant who was key SNCC
> informant is now key BPP informant.

The two Panther groups met and decided to combine. As in Oakland, activists and street brothers joined. The West Siders had solid community support and street experience; the SNCC folks had some political organizing experience. Bobby Rush, one of the SNCC, enlisted 20-year-old Fred Hampton of the Maywood NAACP as a speaker who impressed him. Two months later, October 1968, they had a headquarters at 2350 W. Madison, the heart of the West Side at that time. The building was leased by Bobby Rush and independent South Side alderman Sammy Rayner. Days later, Bob Brown, Rufus "Chakka" Walls, an army veteran and one of the West originators, Drew Ferguson, along with Fred, spoke to a charged-up crowd at the University of Illinois' new Chicago Circle Campus. As news commentator Hugh Hill shouted over the roar of a supercharged crowd, "These Panthers look like they'll be every bit as popular as Oakland!"

**The Spirit of the Times.** The idea of integration had lost steam, but black power was on the move. That is, rather than increase opportunities for black individuals to leave the community and enter the white world, a self-confident spirit would take the entire ghetto to liberation. Malcolm had said the first step toward changing the society was changing the Afro-American's role in it. Free the community from its rulers and restructure it so the old oppressor would not, could not be replaced with a new one. How to go about this? Study!

> ...When you see that you've got a problem, all you have to
> do is examine the historic method used all over the world by
> others who have problems similar to yours. Once you see how
> they got theirs straight, then you know how you can get yours
> straight.
>
> — Malcolm X

Their studies were based on the most popular books on college campuses that decade, those by Marx, Mao, and, for black folks in particular, Franz Fanon. This is where that initial study led them: Capitalism was seen as the culprit in racial oppression. Capitalism, the system of economics based on endless growth and endless competition, something like cancer applied to economics. It was a system that dictated that the big get bigger, even when they are big enough, take more, even when they have taken all they need. The capitalists were known to the Dakota Indians in the 1870s as the Wasichu (those who take everything and more) as they watched them ravage the Black Hills. The same could be said 100 years later. Every industry has to grow, to exploit the world for the sake of its stock investors. It was profit for profit's sake, at the expense of everyone, meaning, for example, that poor people got shoved off their lands when International Harvester invented a new cotton harvester that made them obsolete, that the Navajo got pushed off grazing lands promised them forever when uranium was discovered, or, closer to home, that the Italian community in Chicago got razed when a college campus seemed more profitable. In the atmosphere created by this uncontrolled, unfeeling greed, insecurity abounds among the poor and working class in particular. The go-for-yourself philosophy of individualism—you can make it if you try—made the unsuccessful look for a scapegoat when they individually struggled and failed to achieve the generally unreachable goal of personal economic security. That's where racism came in.

Racism, which had provided a cheap labor force of slaves a century ago, now provided the scapegoat. Why have I failed? Why isn't my life like life on sitcom television—because of the "niggers," or, for blacks, because of those other niggers. Socialism was the answer, with its concern for the group over individual concerns. It was seen as a scientific solution to economic insecurity.

Students had argued over socialism versus capitalism for years, but for the first time in recent history, students—black students—were acting on it. This was a surprise to America's establishment and everyone else; students didn't act in America; they stuffed themselves into phone booths, held panty raids and philosophical discussions. Now, these students acted. (We never shoulda let them niggers in our schools, you could imagine them saying.) It caught our imagination. The Black Panther Party phenomenon spread across the nation, like the invention of television. The ghetto, a colony, the mother country, the United States, black youth, the heroes. It was comparable to the Chinese student movement of 1919, the Algerians under the French. An Algerian, Frantz Fanon, became the new literary leader of the intellectual side of this liberation movement. His book, *The Wretched of the Earth*, gave dramatic insights into the mind of the racially oppressed and their oppressor.

Fanon was educated in Europe, was a success-oriented, white-oriented person who, in the tumultuous times of the Algerian Revolution, forsook his European ways, forsook the rejection of his roots that lay in trying to act white, and returned to his own, the downtrodden, unassimilated Algerians (who did not want to assimilate) to fight a revolution. The analogy for Afro-American students away at white colleges and aware that their cultural outlook was not quite like that of their fellow students was obvious.

*The Wretched of the Earth* describes Fanon's radical personality change, a change that has been the personal side of every social revolution from Chaka of the Zulu through Ché Guevara of Argentina. In this change, a person questions every custom he/she has and analyzes all facets of his or her personality in terms of reshaping it to fit the purposes of the revolution.

Taking a page from Fanon, students like Fred, Bob Brown, and Bobby Rush analyzed the human relationships in society. They looked for ways to make changes in relationships, which produced people who felt guilty about living conditions they did not create, who were aggressive with each other but not with a judge or a landlord, who let the system tell them who they were and how they should act. That role was defined most directly by the society's socializing agents, the police, and indirectly but most persuasively by the media, with its treatment of the poor as deprived, which is at its best sympathy and at its worst contempt, but which in both cases is lacking in respect.

The reality is tough and creates toughness, the ability to survive, to laugh at hardship, to struggle. The people are tough, tough enough to change things if they only see. But life is also rather immediate, doesn't lend opportunity for reflection, change from the norm is dangerous, and so is fairly uncommon—unless there is an overwhelming reason to change. The reality of the 1960s brought that reason to the surface.

The '60s showed the poor and black how the system disrespected them; troubled times brought some of that disrespect out. Yet, even in quiet times, the reason for change is there. For the youth, it can be seen on the corner where the winos waste away or in the old church mothers dying in dirty, thief-ridden nursing homes. Defeat is in the future. The general get-over is not to look at it too hard, to fantasize, get high, get drunk, get the spirit, get anything, but don't get reality. Reality and the defeat it portrays comes and goes like patches of clarity in a mental fog, and in it are the seeds of rebellion. Touch young people with defeatism, and they will reject it. The Party would push the system to show its disrespect blatantly and force the young, the tough, to see that, and they'd work at the response to it.

Until 1968, the rebellion of those who dared to see reality was parasitic, inward rebellion, rebellion that made one a success at the cost of his or her own people. The rebel whose rebellion is the bitter glitter of the crook is self-destructive because in abusing his own people, he erodes his support. Those people are soon out to get him. Similarly, the "good Negro" who makes it by accepting America's disrespect of its non-white is naturally on a self-hate trip. So in 1968, the idea was not only to expose disrespect but to teach a new response to it; don't finesse disrespect and turn it into a profit, don't ignore it, go to war on it! War on it intellectually, scientifically, that was the idea. Don't fantasize, do it! Like Fred forced white kids to deal with their own racism, they would force black kids to deal with racist reality. As Fred said many times, we're dealing with objective reality.

To believe in respect is to affirm it with every action, build the people up where traditions weaken them, where niggers tore one another down, no disrespect of black women by their men, no stealing from the people, no abuse of old black folks, or poor whites for that matter, and no abuse of any of them by "the Man." It was hard and simple, just aggressively interfere, tell the nigger, pimp, policeman, preacher, "No, you can't do that," and if they continue, stop them! Led by this example, the people would do the rest, for they were already tough enough; they just needed the proper example. If CORE had the guts to go into Cicero unarmed or ride mob-hounded buses in Alabama, they would have the guts to stand up on Madison Street and say, "No more of that around here," and back it up with force. It was bold!

No sooner did they open their office doors than that's what they began doing, interfering, stopping pimps, snatching their women and putting them to work selling Panther newspapers, running dope peddlers off Madison, talking about their love for the people, about getting high off just thinking about the people, "All Power to the People," "Death to all oppressors of the unarmed people." It came from Mao and Fanon; they applied it to Chicago.

From a youthful, revolutionary perspective, the black political and economic leaders of 1968 were conservatives who rejected any approach to power that attacked the basic philosophy of the system, though perhaps not consciously so. The leaders wanted in that system, and aside from that, wanted business as usual, pay-offs as usual, patronage as usual. A fine indication of their very real conservatism occurred with the riot of April 1968. Some 2,700 West Siders were arrested, and not one of them was advised to plead for amnesty due to the injustice of the system or make any legal attempt to justify the riot.[14] Not that they didn't feel justified; they were simply not aware of that legal altenative. Now, how could people who act in conformity to the system, who inhibit themselves to fit that system, creatively challenge that system? They couldn't. So the people needed an alternative, to see, at least, a radical alternative. Didn't they have a right to provide it? Wasn't that what democracy was all about?

**The Panthers.** They were attracting the street brothers and sisters, those young men and women who grow up quickly and survive without much family protection. The tough youth, awakening to the beat of the freedom movement. They had seen Dr. King fail in Chicago with their help; now, they wanted to try their way. In the beginning, this seemed to be the ideal organization for them and reflected them. Its politics were blunt, without regard to established power. Borrowing terms from Mao, Marx, and Lenin, they invented words to fit the old terms and breathed the life of the streets into Marx.

The term "liberal," for example, previously referred to moderate whites and allies, but now, based on the Movement's experiences in the '60s, it took on a negative meaning.

This is how Mao Tse-Tung looked at liberalism:

> Liberation manifests itself in various ways...to let things slide
> for the sake of peace and friendship when a person has clearly
> done wrong...to indulge in irresponsible criticism in private
> instead of actively putting forward one's suggestions... To hear
> incorrect views without rebutting them...to see someone harm
> the interests of the masses and yet not feel indignant...to work
> halfheartedly without a definite plan or direction...people
> who are liberals look upon Marxism as abstract dogma. They
> approve of Marxism but are not prepared to practice it...They
> preach Marxism but practice liberalism....

The Panthers translated: A liberal in America was a master of words. Around you, they are all for you, but they can shift for whichever crowd they are with. More importantly, they can always see two equal sides to any situation. If there were 100 Klansmen lynching a black man for eyeballing a white woman, a liberal understands both sides equally. "It's the social climate...be patient, things will get better for your grandchildren...[T]he Klan serves a social function necessary to the oppressed white..." etc. With equal understanding, a liberal cancels action. A liberal does nothing and, by doing nothing, serves the status quo. That's how Gov. Rockefeller of New York, a liberal, let the Attica prison riot end in the slaughter of 41 people by rampaging police. His conscience listened to the complaints of the prisoners, but his heart wasn't in any action. He let the more aggressive, overt racists have their way. In 1968, liberals were saying "peace now," but they booed Panther David Hilliard when he told them, "If you want peace, you have to fight for it!" From the Panther point of view, the kind of peace they wanted was the peace the fox wants, after he's swallowed the chicken.

**Up on Madison, Down on 75th.** What was happening was the college students of the movement were identifying with the street brothers. The students were frustrated with the lack of progress and ready to do whatever it would take to put Afro-American society on the road to active liberation. They'd even risk their lives. "Dare to fight, dare to win!" was the common saying. By reading Fanon and by experience in the Movement, they were feeling ready to implement what Malcolm had taught: Get your freedom by letting the enemy know you'll do anything to get it.

The Panther members and their friends were people, young people from all across the ghetto, people who ordinarily wouldn't come in contact with each other after high school. They were kids up on Madison, heart of the poor ghetto, to down on 75th, where working-class parents warned their kids, "Don't go down there; those niggers mean you no good!" They were from Cabrini-Green Housing projects, fighting to stay out of criminal activities, to Avalon Park, where youngsters had to really try to be as tough as their poorer brothers. They were from the holiness churches and the Episcopal churches, refugees from the hypocrisies of both, from County Jail, from gangs, and from Vietnam. This Panther feeling was a phenomenon that crossed cultural and class lines.

Malcolm had advised in his autobiography, "The most dangerous man in America is the ghetto hustler...the hustler out there in the ghetto jungles has less respect for the white power structure than any other Negro." Ghetto hustlers and anyone else quick-thinking and tough were welcome in the Party, as long as they showed some dedication to black people and were themselves black. After all, white America treated them all the same; why shouldn't they finally work together?

Yet there were differences among them, differences in outlook, in experiences. The children of Chicago's old settlers, who had come in the early part of the century to Chicago, were urbanized Northerners. Their kids actively rejected their own "capitalistic" upbringing in the name of revolution. They read Fanon and Mao, pondered, then acted, maybe. But to the young folks who'd never been urbanized, never been an urban "Negro," the revolution was a reassertion of Afro-American moral values of the South and their rural upbringing. For them, revolution was a gut reaction. The words they used were the same: liberation, revolution, even anti-fascist. But for them, these words meant follow your upbringing to its logical conclusion, fight. While for others, it meant to analyze your actions carefully, follow the political theories of Fanon. Bridging the gap between them, between politician and warrior, was Fred Hampton, a warrior who studied books. Fred obviously recognized the need for both warriors and politicians in the Party. It was Bobby Rush who brought Fred back a second time to speak for the Party, and by January 1969, Fred was at the forefront.

**Discipline.** The youthful Illinois Chapter, set up like Oakland, had a central staff of six. They were the deputy ministers of information, defense, culture, education, finance, and a chairman. The Party had no official leader; rather, these six (later seven) made decisions jointly, with the Chairman as spokesperson. Each minister was responsible for his own group or cadre, as they were called.

Local chapters, like Chicago, were to follow policies initiated in Oakland—for no logical reason except that Huey Newton and Bobby Seale had been the first to think up the idea of a Panther Party and were gutsy enough to confront Oakland's police. (Of course, they had never seen the likes of Chicago's one-party system or how it operated on the black West Side.) Local chapters could appeal decisions made in Oakland, which some said originated in Berkeley, but until that appeal was considered, they were to follow orders. Likewise, individuals in the Illinois Party could appeal local decisions. The idea was from Mao and the Chinese Communist Party and was called democratic centralism. It provided for arguments and yet discipline.

Discipline was strict and often physical. It had to be. The Party had gotten media attention by walking around with guns in California; now, they attracted people who wanted to walk around with guns—youngsters fantasizing.

Discipline was applied democratically. Every member shared work and responsibilities. Everyone, from Chairman to community volunteer, sold Party newspapers and did physical work as well as other responsibilities. Being late for a meeting meant a slap in the face or a kick in the ass, depending on your sex. The Minister of Labor, a new office, got slapped once for being late, and according to her, it worked. A slap in the face or a kick in the ass made the Illinois Party the most effective, most dependable organization she has ever worked for, before or since.

The people running the Party offices, education, culture, and defense were not picked for expertise in the respective fields but because they were leaders. They picked the people they thought could lead. They would have to learn the rest of their jobs.

Because their leaders were admired and because the discipline was strict but fair, they kept a high morale. They were trained by veterans of the war to be tough under police harassment and threats, to have pride, and to recognize their enemy.

**Mile Square and Chicago, Autumn 1968.** High morale and sincerity
are contagious. In Mile Square, it attracted an instant following—
particularly among the youngsters. The Illinois Panthers demanded the
kids discipline themselves to serve the people. They counseled local kids
to stay in school, to stay out of gangs, and away from dope. They babysat
for parents and talked to the older kids of revolution. They grabbed the
local dope dealer and took him into the perpetually flooded basement of
their office, dunked him in the sewer water, then beat him for selling dope
to kids. They did the same with pimps and forced local prostitutes to sell
the Panther paper. Altering the negative mores of the ghetto made them
immediately popular.

They were creating a leadership model for potential liberators in a
community where independent political ideas were violently discouraged.
Twenty-three-fifty W. Madison was in the heart of a community where
police were more abusive, where poverty was the norm, hunger, lead
poisoning, rat bites, and dope were common. Nevertheless, Fred left
Maywood and moved into a building one block south of the office. It was
risky, but it spoke of complete sincerity in the cause of the people. Fred
was unusual, according to everyone who talks about him. His response
to personal crises was different. When he saw someone in trouble, he'd
often risk his own image to step in and settle the problem. He believed
in getting involved in life, yet despite that caring, he was tough, tough
enough to back it up when things got nasty, quick to fight, and good at it.
When the fight was over, and Fred had the advantage, he didn't walk off;
he started to teach as if the fight were simply an opportunity for him to
get his message across: love the people.

Fred was a sensation, the Party was a sensation. In fact, such was
the attraction of the Party, particularly Fred, that scores of youngsters
left home and came to live at Party headquarters. Left home to be like
Fred said, "One hundred percent for the people." It had the aspects of a
youth rebellion. Wherever they went, they captured the imagination of
the young, were cheered, got money and allegiance. They were still only
locally known, yet as the people came over to meet this "bad nigger" Fred,
they were surprised to find, was not the bad nigger, but an intelligent,
good-humored guy who loved to rap and to teach in an entertaining style.
Here, Fred explains his arrest of a Chicago police officer:

Let me give you an example of teaching people. Basically, the way they learn is observation and participation. You know a lot of us go around and joke ourselves and believe the masses have PhDs, but that's not true. And even if they did, it wouldn't make any difference. Because with some things you have to learn by seeing it or either participating in it. And you know yourselves that there are people walking around your community today that have all types of degrees that should be at this meeting but are not here. Right? Because you can have as many degrees as a thermometer. If you don't have any practice, then you can't walk across the street and chew gum at the same time...

Now, let me show you how we're gonna try to do it in the Black Panther Party here. We just got back from the South Side. We went out there—we went out there, and we got to arguing with the pigs, or the pigs got to arguing—he said, "Well, Chairman Fred, you supposed to be so bad, why don't you go and shoot some of those policemen? You always talking about you got your guns and got this; why don't you go shoot some of them?"

And I said, "You've just broken a rule. As a matter of fact, even though you have on a uniform, it doesn't make me any difference. Because I don't care if you got on nine uniforms and 100 badges. When you step outside the realm of legality and into the realm of illegality, then I feel that you should be arrested."

And I told him. "You being what they call the law of entrapment, you tried to incite me to commit a crime, you tried to make me do something that was wrong, you encouraged me, you tried to incite me to shoot a pig. And that ain't cool, brother, you know the law, don't you?"

I told that pig that; I told him, "You got a gun, pig?" I told him, "You gotta get your hands up against the wall. We're gonna do what they call a citizen's arrest." This fool don't know what this is. I said, "Now you be just as calm as you can, and don't make too many quick moves, 'cause we don't have to hit you."

And I told him, like he always told us, I told him, "Well, I'm here to protect you. Don't worry about a thing. I'm here for your benefit." So I sent another brother to call the pigs—you gotta do that in a citizen's arrest. He called the pigs. Here come the pigs with carbines and shotguns, walkin' out there. They came out there talking about how they're gonna arrest Chairman Fred. And I said, "No fool. This is the man you got to arrest. He's the one that broke the law." And what did they do? They bugged their eyes, and they couldn't stand it. You know what they did? They were so mad, they were so angry that they told me to leave.

And what happened? All those people were out there on 63rd Street. What did they do? They were around there laughing and talking with me while I was making the arrest. They looked at me while I was rapping and heard me while I was rapping. So the next time that pig comes on 63rd Street, because of the thing that our Minister of Defense calls observation and participation, that pig might be arrested by anybody.

So what did we do? We were out there educating the people. How did we educate them? Basically, the way people learn; by observation and participation.

If this kind of thing went over well with Afro-American youth, one can also imagine how it went over with the police or with local politicians. Yet they were not the most immediate problem, not yet. The Party hadn't gotten that influential yet. No, the biggest obstacle to the Party's program that winter of 1968 was the youths already organized for the recognition that organization brought, the gangs. The Blackstone Rangers, in particular, were preventing Panther Party members from selling papers in their community. They would first have to deal with the brothers on the block who were harassing them. Fred and the Central Staff's response would be typical—quick and direct!

# Chapter 3

# THE FIRST POLITICAL PROGRAMS OF THE ILLINOIS PANTHERS

**Politicizing the gangs.** The history of gangs in Chicago is probably as old as the city itself. Recorded history goes back at least to the 1870s. Those were the days of fighting "clubs" such as the "Old Hickorys," whose members gave up fighting and became, in time, lawyers, contractors, and aldermen; and they were also the days of more enduring gangs that went into criminal activities, into beer-running, bribery, and murder. These gangs included the Triple Xs (XXX), the Little Murderers, the Aberdeens, the Gloriannas.[15]

The race riot of 1919 was, to some extent, a continuation of hostilities between black and Irish gangs.[16] And in the early 1920s, the Hamburg-Canaryville wars broke out between Irish gangs. Among the Irish, it was said, fighting was a national habit. A brick was commonly referred to as "Irish confetti." Observers of the Irish immigrants said they held a perpetual chip on their shoulders for years of oppression in Ireland at the hands of the English. That was why, or so the saying goes, they made good policemen and politicians. An old poem from Bridgeport went like this:

De furder y' go, de tougher it gets—

I live at Toity-Toid an de tracks

De last house on de corner

And der's blood on de door.[17]

Comparable in more ways than one to an almost forgotten Hamburg-Canaryville war of the '20s was the Englewood-Woodlawn rivalry between the Black Disciples and the Blackstone Rangers, beginning in the early 1960s. It was said these black immigrants had a perpetual chip on their shoulder from years of oppression at the hands of the whites down South. And this was perhaps even more true on the West Side, where Cobras fought Vice Lords.

As the Sixties progressed, some of these fighters would likewise turn from fighting to politics; others would go deeper into crime. Yet, through the Sixties, the war was the thing. The brand of English had changed:

> I'm nemp the demp, the women's pimp

> Women fight for my delight

> I'm the ass-kicker, the city slicker

> The world-shaker, the baby-maker

And the nature of fighting was changed from bricks, chains, and bats to guns, even among youth. The best leader was no longer necessarily the biggest, toughest boxer (though it didn't hurt) but the slick planner, the boy who was good at battle tactics. Still, the need to be somebody in the cold, impersonal poverty of the big city was identical. Gangbangers were mostly ambitious folks. They'd learned at an early age that, being black, their chances of being somebody were slim; being poor and black, even less. Intent on escaping society's label on them as nobodies, they found recognition in notoriety. The "rep" was the thing; to be the baddest motherfucker around.

The U.S. government's recognition of their disruptive power, learned from the rebellions in Detroit, Watts, and Newark, produced money to re-direct the gangs. The fear of rising black nationalism was the impetus. After all, black youths had been immigrants in the 1920s and had fought to climb out of poverty for decades; now, this generation was being infected with the idea that they'd have to liberate the community forcefully. Funds from the U.S. Office of Economic Opportunity, the First National Bank, Sears, the Rockefeller Foundation, and others were now being offered Chicago's exploding black clubs.[18] Meanwhile, youth who joined in civil rights marches who opposed the war in Vietnam— they were getting harassment. It didn't take long for young folks to get the picture: the activists were getting harassed, the gangs funded, federal troops were in the streets that past April, and the King Alfred plan had been "discovered." This was a rumored plan by the federal government to put Afro-Americans into camps, as had been done to Japanese Americans in the 1940s. It looked like the government was getting the black community to war on itself; what was needed was more unity. Even before the crisis between the Panther Party and the Black P. Stone Nation reached a head, the Panthers felt it would be necessary to educate the Stones. The Stones, however, were getting an education of their own.

In the fall of 1967, over fifty youths were shot in gang incidents, and nothing much was done about it. But in the spring of 1968, the Blackstone Rangers faced unusually heavy police attention. Teenagers in the "Stone" communities were being picked up daily by police and dropped off in the heart of Disciple turf. Was this a response to public pressure, or was more subtle political pressure at work? Speculation was that because funds to the Rangers through OEO were not under the control of the Daley machine and because the Rangers were beginning to offer services to the community (as the machine did), that Mayor Daley and company saw the Rangers as competition.[19] After all, Daley's origins were with an Irish "club."

Funding and programs for urban people which didn't come through the "machine" were consistently sensitive issues for the Democratic Party. When, for example, OEO in 1967 had attempted to interfere in the school accountability issue and withheld funds, pressuring the city to provide more community input, the nine legislative members of Congress sent by the machine pressured back in Washington and got the White House to rid the local OEO of its independent-thinking leader.[20] Likewise, the Model Cities program was strategically altered by Senator George Romney (a liberal Democrat) after the program and the Coalition for United Community Action clashed with Mayor Daley and his protege, Irwin France.[21]

The Black P. Stone Nation, formerly the Blackstone Rangers, was becoming political, was doing unusual things for a club. They were recruiting local talent for their own talent show, called "Opportunity Please Knock," which gave exposure to youngsters; they were marching in demonstrations and running youth programs independent of the Democratic Party's control—made possible by federal funding.

In July 1968, the Stones' leaders had been up before a Senate sub-committee, which was trying to discredit the funding programs. They were successful, but the gang's political moves continued. They took up the struggle for allowing black people into the trade unions, and black construction companies got a piece of city construction. Armed with bricks, pipes, and bats, they raided construction sites in the black community and chased big, burly white workers off their jobs— something Jesse Jackson and his people couldn't have done. They went with the Rev. Jackson over to the construction site for the University of Illinois Circle Campus, and when he decided to back off the invasion, they wouldn't permit him, forcing him to go ahead.

The Stones were nevertheless a youthful nation of gang-bangers, wild youth, ready to fight. Some of them went over to Panther Headquarters to see if they could be bullied. They were cool about it, followed protocol; this was, after all, not their turf. The Mile Square brothers in the Party were ready and anxious to return the visit. They felt the Stones, at least those they had seen, were kids playing childish games. They needed an education.

On December 18, 1968, a Party member was shot on P. Stone territory for selling papers there. The word got back to the Panther office, and thirty Panthers grabbed their guns, piled into eight cars, and headed down the Eisenhower Expressway to P. Stone headquarters on 69th and Woodlawn.

Fred, Rush, and the other Panthers went up into the Stones' office and were treated to a weapons display like Red Square, Moscow, on May Day. Approximately 100 boys were brought out on walkie-talkie command, carrying new carbines, shotguns, and pistols. It was impressive but made little effect on them. They'd come to bring a message. They wanted the Stones to end the gang violence and accept the Panther Party's lead in a revolutionary socialist movement. The leaders of the P. Stone Nation claimed they were trying to stop the violence, but felt every bit as educated as the Panther Party and were not interested in socialism. They wanted to make money, not share it. It was classic, tough South Side cynical politics vs. the idealism of Southern-born West Siders.

Chairman Fred told the Stones that the establishment had no place for any independent black organizations, and whether they cleaned up their violence or not, they were facing annihilation, so why not work together? P. Stone agreed but didn't buy the bit about Panther leadership. The Panthers, to them, were just one more group trying to take away their independence. They were expanding now. Once the government gets rid of us, Fred concluded, they will come for you. The Party, in general, realized they were expendable, had no doubts their Party would be destroyed, and that in the way that destruction would come about lay the education that would produce a revolutionary movement among the people.

The city, however, wasn't waiting; they were going for the Stones already. Twenty-three trumped-up arrests of P. Stone leaders, the resultant loss of control over their violence-prone members, which in turn brought an excuse for more police activities against them, were indicators of what was on.

The Panthers tried to achieve a ceasefire between the rival Black Disciples of Englewood and the Stones of Woodlawn. At the same time, police harassment of the P. Stones intensified with help from other service groups like the YMCA, who had a tendency to jealously guard their share of the control over the status quo, questioning why the gangs should be performing services—that was their job! The police department's policies, in terms of P. Stone, seemed to be that they were more concerned with a peace achieved by someone else than with the violence itself. Peace was the job of their newly created Gang Intelligence Unit. This unit, formed just when the largest youth gang in the city (P. Stone) and the largest Afro-American community organization (TWO, The Woodlawn Organization) reached a working agreement, was getting a reputation as some very tough cops. Ed Buckney, the head of Gang Intelligence, expressed his feelings on the gangs in an interview remembered, but not recorded, by the interviewer:

QUESTION: How can other social agencies work with gangs?

BUCKNEY: They can't.

QUESTION: Then who can work with the gangs?

BUCKNEY: The police.

QUESTION: How can churches and other groups help the police work with gangs?

BUCKNEY: They can't.

QUESTION: Of the many different efforts now being made in Chicago to deal with gangs, which has been the most helpful to the police?

BUCKNEY: The formation of the Gang Intelligence Unit.

QUESTION: What can be done about the gangs?

BUCKNEY: They must be broken up.[22]

Gang members should not be allowed to do things for youth, was what the other agencies said. The press, at least the *Tribune*, was suddenly outraged that gang members ran job programs. The *"Trib"* printed stories on its front page of supposed sex orgies and other illegal acts at the job program site. The fact that the police never arrested anyone for these acts, each supposedly committed by a named person with a supposed eyewitness, indicates how invalid the stories were.

And now Jesse Jackson was suddenly concerned about gang violence. Although he'd sought them out earlier for help, now he formed a group called Black Men Moving to protect the community from the gangs. The Panthers said the federal government had gotten to Rev. Jackson and told him to drop any association with the gangs or lose federal funds. The Panther Party ran an article on him, labeling him the government's top flunky and best bootlicker. The Panther Party was never "liberal" in its criticism.

Black power was on the rise, but who in the community would get it was the question. The Panthers saw themselves at one end on the scale, pushing for "all power to the people," the moderates pushed for more power to the "right kind" of people. More accurately, it seems the Panther Party wanted power for the politically powerless, with themselves at the vanguard of that group (which was most of black Chicago). Rev. Jackson screened his own position behind a mountain of rhetoric. "I am somebody!" was his expression. And the Party put it to him, "Who are you?" They weren't intimidated by the establishment, and that was their attraction to the young. How you gonna do anything creative in a state of perpetual insecurity like the moderates? And so, many of the moderate leaders' own youth supported the Panther Party.

The Panther Party's moves were original, unpredictable, and they had a following among the youth. The question in the mind of the white establishment probably was: What would they do next?

The FBI wasn't waiting to see. The local FBI saved a local criminal from serving time in jail and told him to enlist in the Black Panther Party for them. He was there when the Party opened its doors on Madison and Western, and his name was William O'Neal. O'Neal related the meetings of the "Stones" and the Panthers to his FBI chief, Roy Mitchell. O'Neal thought he was being "slick," playing both sides of the revolution, trying to impress his friends in the Panther Party with the cash he secretly got from the FBI. Meanwhile, the FBI used O'Neal in their first attempt to destroy Fred Hampton.

They found out that the Panthers were not a violence-prone group, though they talked about it, and that the "Stones" were. They decided to see if they could use the "Stones" to destroy the Panther Party. The FBI drafted a letter to P. Stone leader Jeff Fort, which appeared to come from a member of the Panther Party. The letter read as follows:

> Brother Jeff:
>
> I've spent some time with some Panther friends on the west
> side lately and I know what's been going on. The brothers
> that run the Panthers blame you for blocking their thing and
> there's supposed to be a hit out for you. I'm not a Panther, or a
> Ranger, just black. From what I see these Panthers are out for
> themselves not black people. I think you ought to know what
> they're up to. I know what I'd do if I was you. You might hear
> from me again.
>
> A black brother you don't know.[23]

A memo from the FBI in Chicago to the Washington office explains the purpose:

> It is believed the above (letter) may intensify the degree of
> animosity between the two groups and occasion Fort to take
> retaliatory action which could disrupt the BPP or lead to
> reprisals against its leadership.
>
> Consideration has been given to a similar letter to the BPP
> alleging a Ranger plot against the BPP leadership; however,
> it is not felt this would be productive principally because
> the BPP at present is not believed as violence prone as the
> Rangers, to whom violent type activity—shooting and the
> like—is second nature.[24]

It didn't work because Fred got wind of the letter and called up
Fort, telling him it was a plant by the police or somebody. But O'Neal
continued to work at increasing distrust between the two groups. And
when another Panther feared he wasn't trusted and possibly related it to
O'Neal, the FBI had another letter ready. This one read:

> Brother Hampton,
>
> Just a word of warning. A Stone friend tells me [name deleted]
> wants the Panthers and is looking for someone to get you out
> of the way. Brother Jeff is supposed to be interested. I'm just
> a black man looking for blacks working together, not more of
> this gang-banging.

Yet another letter was sent, this time to the leader of the Mau Mau, a
self-defense group that had joined the Party en mass and was consequently
having trouble following Party orders.

> Brother Kenyatta,
>
> I'm from the south side and have some Panther friends that
> know you and tell me what's been going on. I know these
> two _____ that run the Panthers for a long time and those
> mothers been with every black outfit going where it looked
> like they was something in it for themselves. I heard too they're
> sweethearts and that _____ has worked for the man, that's why

he's not in Viet Nam. Maybe that's why they're just playing
like real Panthers. I hear a lot of the brothers are with you and
want those mothers out but don't know how. The Panthers
need real black men for leaders not freaks. Don't give up
brothers.


A black friend.


The FBI's Chicago office was turning out black fiction like "Iceberg
Slim." And the mail to and from Washington was crowded with credit-
seeking for Panthers killed, run out of town, divorced or fired, from
San Diego to New York. In Chicago, they asked for a bonus for their
local "informant." O'Neal had prevented an alliance between the Illinois
Panther Party and the Conservative Vice Lords. He had terrorized
innocent people, had told the FBI which Panther leaders were leaving the
city and at what time, so the local police could harass them. However, in
Chicago, they couldn't get anyone killed or destroy the Party's morale. In
fact, when one of their prize informants in the East, George Sams, came
to Chicago, he got a good beating at Panther headquarters for not giving
them straight answers. They didn't know for sure if he was a spy, but they
knew a liar when they heard one and dealt with it "Panther fashion."

Negotiations with the Rangers did little to get allegiance from them.
The P. Stone Nation wanted to maintain its independence and its profits,
and they wanted no one telling them not to. Yet, when, in the next
few months, the police began to harass the Panther Party and the Party
responded with armed defense, the message went out to all the youth
gangs across the city. For a while, they fought and killed each other and
thought nothing of beating or killing innocent people; they steered clear
of the police. So if the Panthers took on the police, they got respect. It
was felt they'd take on anyone.

Suspicions, meanwhile, were beginning to surround William O'Neal,
who had messed over the truce plans pretty effectively. Billy Brooks,
known as Ché, was one of the first. Ché was the silent, mean-looking,
quiet type who studied people with a steady, icy stare, deep-set eyes in a
dark face, behind an Indian nose. In fact, Ché's stare was of some concern
to Fred, who was known to say, "Ché, how we going to make alliances
and you sitting there with that look?" But Ché not only stared for effect,
he was observant. And, late January, he accused O'Neal of being a pig and

demanded he be expelled.

O'Neal, however, was the responsibility of Bobby Rush, the Deputy Minister of Defense—as each minister had his own cadre. Rush considered the accusation, found it unsupported by concrete evidence, and kept him. So O'Neal got away with it for now. Yet Fred took to using Cleve Cook as his bodyguard rather than O'Neal. O'Neal was too slick, too shifty.

Meanwhile, on the West Side, the Conservative Vice Lords also saw the Panthers as a threat to their turf. Rumors said that CVL had shot up the front window of the Panther headquarters. CVL, like the P. Stone Nation, had just received a large federal grant and was using it to set up businesses on West 16th Street. They wanted no one competing for "their" street—where the Panther Party already had one free breakfast program and was planning a free medical clinic. The Vice Lords told the Panthers, "No way we letting you have that medical clinic!" To which Fred dramatically replied in a speech, "I guess having a free medical clinic for the masses, for the people, is worth 8-10 dead Vice Lords."

The Panthers failed to get an alliance with the Vice Lords, but in fact, something much deeper had occurred between the gangs and the Panthers. That infection of black self-respect, the positive mood, had rubbed off. Moreover, the Panthers showed the gangs up, for while the gangs were tough and violent with each other and with innocent people, they left the "man" alone. Caught on the wrong side of the law by agents of the law, their position was weak.

On the other hand, the Panthers believed in what they were doing; when harassed by the police for doing nothing illegal, why they responded strongly. It was a powerful psychological message—they were sincere.

**Leaders of the Midwest Radicals.** Chicago's Panther Party was a sound organization in contrast to other Panther chapters. And, Oakland began using Chicago's most valuable leaders to go all across the Midwest, weed out government informants, and set chapters straight. One of their first trips was to Detroit, a trip Fred made with Field Lieutenant Jewell Cook and Chaka. Armed with the name of one Panther and a phone number, they found him and forced him to bring everyone else together and start talking. The place evidently was crowded with informants, some of whom didn't know they were informing on other informants. The Chicago boys tested the commitment of each suspected informant by getting them to take some "revolutionary" action and checking their stories out, then left the Detroit Panther Party in the hands of the few they could rely on. It had been a tough job, coming into a strange city, going down to Wayne State University, armed and shaking up a few people, but they accomplished what they set out to do. After that trip, in fact, no one of the street toughs in the Party doubted Fred's ability to lead them.

The Field Lieutenant led another cadre of Party members to Cleveland, including William O'Neal. Cleveland had a fairly good organization; his biggest headache there had been O'Neal. In fact, O'Neal seemingly tried to take charge, but when his bluff was called, he backed down. These trips became common for Party members, and it was soon clear Oakland was using Chicago to run the Midwest.

**Politics and Free Breakfast.** As the spring of '69 began, the Panther Party was still increasing in size and effectiveness. It was perhaps 1,000 strong and was becoming active across the city, beginning to serve people on a wider scale. Party headquarters was a center for many youth groups, an educational center in revolutionary politics where members and community volunteers went through six-week courses in Marxist politics, which were, more accurately, Panthers relating street realities in Marxist language, applying the Panther Party's formal ten-point program [see pages 46-49], Marxism never stuck well. It was too dry, too analytical. Panther teachers, for example, had trouble with the idea that they were members of the *Lumpen* proletariat. Scientific socialism didn't mix with their natural religious orientation. The basic message made sense; however, a program for liberation. They were implementing a program that would change people's lives. And they put the program ahead of any personality. They were not about electing a man; they were about implementing a program.

Classes required homework, and their homework was to read the *Autobiography of Malcolm X*, *The Wretched of the Earth*, by Fanon, and *The Quotations of Chairman Mao Tsetung*. With their increasing workload, this reading was not always done. Yet they did discuss and argue over Fanon. Meanwhile, life in the city streets was a practical reality that took precedence and couldn't be ignored. Yet, for the cold city streets of Chicago and its one-party state, they were given nothing to read. As of '69, Avard Strickland's *History of the Chicago Urban League* was out, and Ovid DeMaris' *Captive City*, which revealed much of how city politics

## Black Panther Party 10-Point Platform and Program

**1. We Want Freedom. We Want Power to Determine the Destiny of Our Black Community.**

We believe that Black people will not be free until we are able to determine our destiny.

**2. We Want Full Employment for Our People.**

We believe that the federal government is responsible and obligated to give every man employment or a guaranteed income. We believe that if the White American businessmen will not give full employment, then the means of production should be taken from the businessmen and placed in the community so that the people of the community can organize and employ all of its people and give a high standard of living.

**3. We Want An End to the Robbery By the CAPITALIST of Our Black Community.**

We believe that this racist government has robbed us, and now we are demanding the overdue debt of forty acres and two mules. Forty acres and two mules were promised 100 years ago as restitution for slave labor and mass murder of Black people. We will accept the payment in currency which will be distributed to our many communities. The Germans are now aiding the Jews in Israel for the genocide of the Jewish people. The Germans murdered six million Jews. The American racist has taken part in the slaughter of over fifty million Black people; therefore, we feel that this is a modest demand that we make.

**4. We Want Decent Housing Fit For The Shelter of Human Beings.**

We believe that if the White Landlords will not give decent housing to our Black community, then the housing and the land should be made into cooperatives so that our community, with government aid, can build and make decent housing for its people.

October 1966
Black Panther Party
Platform and Program

# What We Want
# What We Believe

Huey P. Newton  Minister of Defense
Black Panther Party

1. We want freedom. We want power to determine the destiny of our Black Community.

We believe that black people will not be free until we are able to determine our destiny.

2. We want full employment for our people.

We believe that the federal government is responsible and obligated to give every man employment or a guaranteed income. We believe that if the white American businessmen will not give full employment, then the means of production should be taken from the businessmen and placed in the community so that the people of the community can organize and employ all of its people and give a high standard of living.

3. We want an end to the robbery by the CAPITALIST of our Black Community.

We believe that this racist government has robbed us and now we are demanding the overdue debt of forty acres and two mules. Forty acres and two mules was promised 100 years ago as restitution for slave labor and mass murder of black people. We will accept the payment in currency which will be distributed to our many communities. The Germans are now aiding the Jews in Israel for the genocide of the Jewish people. The Germans murdered six million Jews. The American racist has taken part in the slaughter of over fifty million black people; therefore, we feel that this is a modest demand that we make.

4. We want decent housing, fit for shelter of human beings.

We believe that if the white landlords will not give decent housing to our black community, then the housing and the land should be made into cooperatives so that our community, with government aid, can build and make decent housing for its people.

5. We want education for our people that exposes the true nature of this decadent American society. We want education that teaches us our true history and our role in the present-day society.

We believe in an educational system that will give to our people a knowledge of self. If a man does not have knowledge of himself and his position in society and the world, then he has little chance to relate to anything else.

6. We want all black men to be exempt from military service.

We believe that Black people should not be forced to fight in the military service to defend a racist government that does not protect us. We will not fight and kill other people of color in the world who, like black people, are being victimized by the white racist government of America. We will protect ourselves from the force and violence of the racist police and the racist military, by whatever means necessary.

7. We want an immediate end to POLICE BRUTALITY and MURDER of black people.

We believe we can end police brutality in our black community by organizing black self-defense groups that are dedicated to defending our black community from racist police oppression and brutality. The Second Amendment to the Constitution of the United States gives a right to bear arms. We therefore believe that all black people should arm themselves for self-defense.

8. We want freedom for all black men held in federal, state, county and city prisons and jails.

We believe that all black people should be released from the many jails and prisons because they have not received a fair and impartial trial.

9. We want all black people when brought to trial to be tried in court by a jury of their peer group or people from their black communities, as defined by the Constitution of the United States.

We believe that the courts should follow the United States Constitution so that black people will receive fair trials. The 14th Amendment of the U.S. Constitution gives a man a right to be tried by his peer group. A peer is a person from a similar economic, social, religious, geographical, environmental, historical and racial background. To do this the court will be forced to select a jury from the black community from which the black defendant came. We have been, and are being tried by all-white juries that have no understanding of the "average reasoning man" of the black community.

10. We want land, bread, housing, education, clothing, justice and peace. And as our major political objective, a United Nations-supervised plebiscite to be held throughout the black colony in which only black colonial subjects will be allowed to participate, for the purpose of determining the will of black people as to their national destiny.

When, in the course of human events, it becomes necessary for one people to dissolve the political bands which have connected them with another, and to assume, among the powers of the earth, the separate and equal station to which the laws of nature and nature's God entitle them, a decent respect to the opinions of mankind requires that they should declare the causes which impel them to the separation.

We hold these truths to be self-evident, that all men are created equal; that they are endowed by their Creator with certain unalienable rights; that among these are life, liberty, and the pursuit of happiness. That, to secure these rights, governments are instituted among men, deriving their just powers from the consent of the governed, that, whenever any form of government becomes destructive of these ends, it is the right of the people to alter or to abolish it, and to institute a new government, laying its foundation on such principles, and organizing its powers in such form, as to them shall seem most likely to effect their safety and happiness. Prudence, indeed, will dictate that governments long established should not be changed for light and transient causes; and, accordingly, all experience hath shown, that mankind are more disposed to suffer, while evils are sufferable, than to right themselves by abolishing the forms to which they are accustomed. But, when a long train of abuses and usurpations, pursuing invariably the same object evinces a design to reduce them under absolute despotism, it is their right, it is their duty, to throw off such government, and to provide new guards for their future security.

## 5. We Want Education for Our People That Exposes The True Nature Of This Decadent American Society.

We Want Education That Teaches Us Our True History And Our Role in the Present-Day Society. We believe in an educational system that will give to our people a knowledge of self. If a man does not have knowledge of himself and his position in society and the world then he has little chance to relate to anything else.

**6. We Want All Black Men To Be Exempt From Military Service.**

We believe that Black people should not be forced to fight in the military service to defend a racist government that does not protect us. We will not fight and kill other people of color in the world who, like Black people, are being victimized by the White racist government of America. We will protect ourselves from the force and violence of the racist police and the racist military by whatever means necessary.

**7. We Want An Immediate End to POLICE BRUTALITY and the MURDER of Black People.**

We believe we can end police brutality in our Black community by organizing Black self-defense groups that are dedicated to defending our Black community from racist police oppression and brutality. The Second Amendment to the Constitution of the United States gives a right to bear arms. We, therefore, believe that all Black people should arm themselves for self-defense.

**8. We Want Freedom For All Black Men Held in Federal, State, County and City Prisons and Jails.**

We believe that all Black People should be released from the many jails and prisons because they have not received a fair and impartial trial.

**9. We Want All Black People When Brought to Trial To Be Tried In Court By A Jury Of Their Peer Group Or People From Their Black Communities, As Defined By the Constitution of the United States.**

We believe that the courts should follow the United States Constitution so that Black people will receive fair trials. The Fourteenth Amendment of the U.S. Constitution gives a man a right to be tried by his peer group. A peer is a person from a similar economic, social, religious, geographical, environmental, historical, and racial background. To do this the court will be forced to select a jury from the Black community from which the Black defendant came. We have been, and we are being, tried by all-White juries that have no understanding of the "average reasoning man" of the Black community.

**10.   We Want Land, Bread, Housing, Education, Clothing, Justice And Peace.**

When, in the course of human events, it becomes necessary for one people to dissolve the political bands which have connected them with another, and to assume, among the powers of the earth, the separate and equal station to which the laws of nature and nature's God entitle them, a decent respect of the opinions of mankind requires that they should declare the causes which impel them to the separation.

We hold these truths to be self-evident, that all men are created equal; that they are endowed by their Creator with certain inalienable rights; that among these are life, liberty, and the pursuit of happiness. **That, to secure these rights, governments are instituted among men, deriving their just powers from the consent of the governed; that, whenever any form of government becomes destructive of these ends, it is the right of the people to alter or abolish it, and to institute a new government, laying its foundation on such principles, and organizing its powers in such form, as to them shall seem most likely to effect their safety and happiness.** Prudence, indeed, will dictate that governments long established should not be changed for light and transient causes; and, accordingly, all experience hath shown that mankind are more disposed to suffer, while evils are sufferable, than to right themselves by abolishing the forms to which they are accustomed. **But, when a long train of abuses and usurpations, pursing invariably the same object, evinces a design to reduce them under absolute despotism, it is their right, it is their duty, to throw off such government, and to provide new guards for their future security.**

worked, was on the market. Both would have been valuable. Oakland's leadership had them relating to the international scene, but at home they were on their own.

As George Dunne, president of the Cook County Board, said, "A political organization depends on giving service to the people." The members of the Panther Party began serving the people as if they'd read Dunne, but it was Mao who was their source of inspiration.

The idea of serving the people was why, in April, the first Free Breakfast for Children Program opened at the Better Boys Foundation on Pulaski Avenue, north of 16th Street. Better Boys had resisted, but Fred and the Party argued and threatened until they gave in. Free breakfasts were an Oakland idea, based on a survey of the black community there, but the need was as applicable to Chicago. Their political message in the program was two-fold: (1) we, the young adults of the community, will find a way to feed our own, and (2) we will expose to the people of the community what the richest nation in the world has failed to guarantee to its citizens. Being fed, they said, was a right all children should have. Within a year, the government would respond with a free lunch program.

The Party searched high and low for more community centers willing to allow them, "notoriously militant Negroes," the opportunity to feed children. Not surprisingly, the local black Protestant churches generally closed their doors to the idea. One black church on the edge of the Henry Horner Housing complex had never even had a resident of that housing project as a member, much less thought of serving the community's needs. The Catholic churches, on the other hand, welcomed the Panther breakfast programs. The white priests at St. Dominic's in Cabrini-Green allowed the Panthers the use of their church for movies, forums, and rallies as well. They, the Catholic priests, seemed to respond to the idea of kids getting food, of young adults serving youths, ignoring the politics.

When the Panthers hit the pavement looking for food donations, however, it was the local black (and some white) businessmen who responded most enthusiastically—the same businessmen labeled in the Marxist theories as "avaricious businessmen" or "pork-chop capitalists." Children at a Panther breakfast site often ate free Parker House surplus sausages, Oscar Meyer meat, and drank free Joe Louis Milk. A people's program of service did something for the community which no government program could: It gave the people release from the attitude that they were government dependents and gave community leaders the opportunity to support this self-help attitude.

By the end of May 1969, the Chicago Panthers had expanded their program all across the city. They served free breakfast for children at the Marcy Center on 16th and Hamlin, at the People's Church at 201 S. Ashland, at Precious Blood Church on Congress and Western, at the Madden Center near 22nd and State, on 35th Street near Indiana, on 45th Street near State, and at their office on Madison and Western, as well as at those sites previously mentioned. Robert Lucas, former head of CORE in Chicago, whom the FBI was trying to pit against the Panthers, had been won over by their successes. He held a news conference commending them for feeding almost 4,000 kids daily without a cent of government money or government controls.[25]

In the Chicago ghettos, from Princeton Park to Cabrini-Green, from Altgeld Gardens to Austin, little kids have grown up, like kids everywhere else, admiring the big boys and girls, their older brothers and sisters, the young adults of the community. But in the inner city, they have often grown up with the feeling that being black and poor, they are nobodies. Against that feeling comes the cry: I am somebody! The preacher cries, "I am somebody! I am somebody because I love the Lord; Mayor Daley doesn't know me, but somebody greater does!" And in the very stubbornness of his cry comes the sneaking suspicion that he, too, feels he's nobody. Children pick it up semi-consciously. It creeps into their psyche as they are being ignored by an overworked mother and seldom-seen daddy. They look for big brother and big sister, but where are they? They are out hustling, getting the cash and flash to prove to the world the worth of their lives. Unfortunately, the flashiest are often pimping or selling dope—because of their ambition and the lack of opportunities to be straight and hold regular jobs. This is, of course, a lot of generalizing. A lot of kids are immune to flash and cash because Momma does have time, Daddy is home, or because they have a minister, uncle, or big brother who is square. Yet the pattern is there. It has become traditional—except in the years 1968-1974—for some 4,000 kids, every working day, they looked up and saw their heroes serving them free breakfasts, not pimping, but busting pimps. They were getting the idea they were some special people. I must be somebody; Fred is serving my breakfast. Not only that, but him 'n Willie and Ché snatched a pimp off the streets yesterday, beat him, took his girls, and had them selling Panther papers, raising money for my breakfast. It was a revolutionary thought—teaching by example.

Education through participation was the political idea in '69, and
Fred put it like this:

> Our Breakfast for Children program is feeding a lot of
> children, and the people understand our Breakfast for
> Children program. We sayin' something like this —we saying
> that theory's cool, but theory with no practice ain't shit. You
> got to have both of them—the two go together. We have a
> theory about feeding kids free. What'd we do? We put it into
> practice. That's how people learn. A lot of people don't know
> how serious the thing is. They think the children we feed ain't
> really hungry. I don't know five-year-old kids that can act well,
> but I know that if they not hungry, we sure got some actors.
> We got five-year-old actors that could take the academy award.
> Last week, they had a whole week dedicated to the hungry in
> Chicago. Talkin' about the starvation rate here that went up
> 15%. Over here, where everybody should be eating. Why?
> Because of capitalism.
>
> What are we doing? The Breakfast for Children program. We
> are running it in a socialist manner. People came and took
> our program, saw it in a socialist fashion, not even knowing
> it was socialism. People are gonna take our program and tell
> us to go on to a higher level. They gonna take our program
> and work it in a socialist manner. What'd the pig say? He say,
> "Nigger, that program is a socialistic program." "I don't give a
> fuck if it's Communism. You put your hands on that program
> motherfucker, and I'll blow your motherfucking brains out."
> And he knew it. We been educating him, not by reading
> matter, but through observation and participation. By letting
> him come in and work our program. Not theory and theory
> alone, but theory and practice. The two go together. We not
> only thought about Marxist-Leninist theory—we put it into
> practice. This is what the Black Panther Party is about.[26]

**The Rainbow Coalition.** On a cool May evening, as the north wind
blustered down Wells Avenue, blowing particles of dust in swirls around
the fancy gateways and high brick fences of the rather exclusive Near

North neighborhood, Lucy Montgomery's phone rang. There was a storm brewing, and it was not from the Canadian Rockies. It was from the West Side of Chicago. She answered the phone, and a male voice said, "Lucy Montgomery?" "Yes," she replied. "This is Fred Hampton of the Illinois Black Panther Party. Can we come talk with you?"

The Rainbow Coalition was beginning, and Fred had done his homework. He was establishing contacts with the people of the North Side to find out what services the people outside the ghetto had and what they needed. He began by telling Lucy so much about herself that she was startled. Gossip and rumors were seldom accurate. Lucy was a veteran of the civil rights movement and a supporter of SDS. Was she in touch with the social service programs offered among various people on the North Side was what Fred wanted to know. She invited him over, and he and his cadre came, questioning her in their attempts to develop a program that reached out from the ghetto to achieve solidarity with other communities. Revolutionary Fred realized what traditional black politicians did not— minority politics means coalition politics. The Panther Party felt it could be the vanguard in a coalition that introduced socialism to the city. Lucy liked Fred, Ché, Doc, and Jewell. They were, to her, a wealthy socialite, tough but not cold, sincere and confident, the kind of people that could be trusted.

The Party politicized a Puerto Rican club called the Young Lords. Now the Young Lords began a free breakfast for children program of their own. Panther Field Marshal Bob Lee, a student of the writings of Saul Alinsky, worked in Uptown with an Appalachian club called the Young Patriots. Here, too, the Panthers successfully achieved an alliance, and these fellows, who wore the Confederate flag on their jackets, began serving the children of Uptown free breakfasts and eventually other services. In the Rogers Park neighborhood was a club known as Rising Up Angry, a club that had the traditional "greaser" image—black leather jackets, jeans, motorcycles. They allied with the Party, creating a comic book that preached people power and poked fun at "da Mayor."

"You don't fight fire with fire!" Fred said, "And you don't fight racism with more racism!"

Moves the Party made to align with "intellectual" whites had less positive results. The cultural gap was wider. Part of the problem was the guilt the "haves" imposed on themselves, and their lack of sincerity— and the street response to guilt. "Yeah, we say we'd try to raise some 'bread' for you guys, but we didn't mean for sure..." "Listen!" the brother would interrupt, grabbing the student, "Y'all raise that motherfuckin' cash or take an ass licking!" And he'd be serious! While this method sometimes worked, in it lay the excuses to leave the struggle for people not really interested but feeling guilty about their own lifestyles.

Sheltered rich kids who didn't think rough kids had the sensitivity to see through them got their eyes opened quick. The Chicago Seven defendants ignored Fred when he told them not to clown before Judge Hoffman. Hoffman, said Fred, was the city's lynching judge and he read for them the judge's record. The defendants nodded and smiled but weren't listening. They were sneaking out to the kitchen, one at a time, to eat and get drunk. For a time, the Panthers observed their allies, then decided to return the bad manners; they stormed the kitchen and helped themselves. Those rich kids were sincere, learned how to be like their rougher brothers—learned to be blunt, aggressive and, above all, hard-working. Some of the others got frustrated with the hard work and went off. They were called the Weathermen, and they came to Chicago with a plan to run wild in the streets in September 1969. Fred told them to dump the plan and educate the people; that was more important— if duller. Mark Rudd then told Fred he doubted if the Panthers, Fred included, were really revolutionaries if they avoided violence. Fred's response was to "fire him up" (hopefully re-educating him). Nevertheless, the effort of Fred was wasted. The Weathermen went on what Fred called their "Custeristic venture" (referring to General Custer at the Little Bighorn) through the streets of the Near North Side.

Handling a coalition was difficult, yet Fred recognized that the Party itself was a coalition environment, the black community, a community of a variety of backgrounds, and if they could handle that, why not break down all the barriers that separated people? Love for the (average) people was the message (excluding the police), and they could use it to dismantle the Machine-ruled city politics.

A political party is run basically by hard work, according to George Dunne. A Panther member's day was a good example. The dedicated ones put in fourteen to sixteen hours, seven days a week. It was becoming a full commitment without pay. They were working, eating, and sleeping with the Party's ten-point program on their minds and how to take the program to the people. Holding jobs became too time-consuming; outside interests melted away. More and more, they relied on their ability to get donations. They were sometimes taking in $1,000 per week, according to Bobby Rush later, though they kept very poor records. Maybe sixty percent of their money went to the free breakfasts or toward the proposed free medical center. The remainder went on rent, utilities, and food. They neglected health care, clothing, and sleep. What mattered were the program and the people.

They preached socialism and revolution:

> Some people talk a lot about communism, but the people can't understand and progress to the stage of communism right away or because of abstract arguments. They say you got to crawl before you can walk. And, the Black Panther Party, as the vanguard party, thought that the Breakfast for Children Program was the best technique of crawling that any vanguard party could follow. And we got a whole lot of folks that's going to be walking. And then a whole lot of folks that's gonna be running. And when you get that, what you got? You got a whole lot of PIGS that's gonna be running. That's what our program's about.

> The Black Panther Party is about the complete revolution. We not gonna go out there and half do a thing. And you can let the pigs know it. They come here and hide—they so uncomfortable, they sitting on a tape recorder, they got their gun in their hair—they got to hide all this shit, and they come here and do all this weird action. All they got to do is come up to 2350 West Madison any day of the week, and anybody up there'll let them know, let the motherfucker know: Yes, we subversive. Yes, we subversive with the bullshit we are confronted with today. Just as subversive as anybody can be subversive. And we think them motherfuckers is the criminals. They the ones always hiding. We the ones up in front. We're out in the open, these motherfuckers should start wearing uniforms. They want to know if the Panthers are goin' underground—these motherfuckers IS underground. You can't find 'em. People call the pigs but nobody knows where they at. They're out chasing us.

They hiding—can't nobody ever see 'em.

> When people got a problem, they come to the Black Panther
> Party for help and that's good. Because, like Mao says, we are
> supposed to be ridden by the people, and Huey says we're
> going to be ridden down the path of social revolution, and
> that's for the people. The people ought to know that the Black
> Panther Party is one thousand percent for the People. They
> write a lot of articles, you know, niggers'll run up to you in a
> minute—when I say niggers I mean white niggers and black
> niggers alike—niggers'll run up to you and talk that shit about,
> "Man, I read in the *Tribune* today." Well, you say, 'Man,' fuck
> it right there. If you didn't read it in the BLACK PANTHER
> paper, in the MOVEMENT—then you ain't read shit.[27]

The speeches were great, the times of confrontation exciting, but
again the grease that made it all come together was the work. Walking the
streets selling the Panther paper, arguing with the people, avoiding the
traps local politicians laid for them, getting donations for their programs,
seeking out sites, speaking to youth groups about how they should "Serve
the people, get high off the love of the people"—it went on day in and
day out, and the people took to it. Serving the people became a sort of
fad. (I remember once stopping my car in the middle of King Drive
and 63rd, picking up an old drunken woman lying in the street, and
taking her to the hospital (Billings) because the Panthers had pricked my
conscience with that idea.)

In the midst of this activity, the strain of their workload came the
inevitable police harassment. They had challenged the police, challenged
even the federal government, and the response they got? Well, they didn't
quite expect -it—at least not quite the way it came.

In January 1969, the FBI got the Chicago police to arrest Fred, on
behalf of the Maywood police, for that old trumped-up ice cream truck
robbery charge. They timed it to happen just as Fred reached a local radio
station where host Howard Miller was to interview him on citywide and
beyond radio. Not only did the arrest embarrass the Party, but it blocked
Fred from communicating with a wider audience. When Fred was bailed
out, he told the others on staff that the police told him, "You'd better
stop, better knock it off, or we'll kill you!" Fred was ready for the police,

but clearly, he didn't know who was pulling the strings that made them so efficient to arrest him at the correct time—or set him up for something worse. The Panther Party in 1969 simply did not know how many and how great in power their enemies were and didn't realize how far those people would go. The police, perhaps, they could handle, for the police and Chicago politicians are often their own worst enemies.

# Chapter 4

# THE CHICAGO POLICE IN THE LATE 1960s

**Patrolmen, tough or brutal?** Disgusted with his former life, Walter Smith [name changed here] left the gang scene to join the good guys, and in 1966, at the age of 22, became a Chicago police officer. One of his first experiences on the beat occurred the fall of 1966. He and his partner, a ten-year veteran, were chasing a speeding auto down Sacramento Avenue. The red convertible darted in and around traffic through a red light at Fullerton, heading south at 60 m.p.h., with the police right behind. Three kids were in the car, Puerto Ricans.

The car swerved to avoid a collision, skidded up on the sidewalk, and got stuck between a hydrant and a "mercado." The three boys tumbled out, springing to their feet running. One, the driver, was too slow. The veteran officer caught him, slammed him into the narrow gangway between two stores. The big veteran, about six feet, 220 pounds, took his night stick and plunged it into the skinny kid's stomach. He turned his head, yelling back to Walter, "Wally, call for help." Walter didn't see the need, but he called anyway while his partner got in two more licks. Two minutes later, another squad car pulled up. The veteran invited the two officers over. One patrolman knocked a tooth loose with a gloved fist, the other crashed a blow to his ribs. By now, the scene had spectators shouting for them to stop it. It might as well have been a cheering section. "C'mon, Wally, get your licks in," his partner urged. Walter was a little shaken, "No, you guys handle it." His partner noted the look on Walter's face as they threw the kid into the wagon. "Look, Wally," he said, taking him aside, "this cocksucker here is gonna have a white shirt, a tie, a priest and a mother when he goes before the judge. He's gonna get his wrist slapped, maybe. This way, we teach them up front, ya see?" Walter saw alright, but it made him wonder; his partner wasn't a bad guy, so what did the rougher cops do if this was so casual?[28]

The Chicago Police Department in 1968 was approximately 10,000 strong. It administered the law through 26 district police stations. In addition, there were six task forces, described as mobile units which could cross district lines without clearance from a station. They had gained a reputation as rough cops—macho police. From these six task forces, a special unit was created in 1968 to deal with the new phenomenon in the Afro-American community of huge gangs and explosive gang wars. It was the Gang Intelligence Unit.

The Chicago Police Department had also been politicized and radicalized by the disturbances of the civil rights movement of 1963-67. That is to say, many of the patrolmen, being white residents of the very neighborhoods the civil rights marchers walked through, found civil rights a threat and black activists their enemies. Some officers quit rather than protect demonstrators; others did the job reluctantly. Both their racism and their conservatism were heightened.

Overall, relationships between the Afro-American ghetto and the police grew worse. As the urban ghettoes became more politicized and the people in them more impatient with the overt racist reactions to them, the police were most directly affected, though they hadn't created the conditions there. As one policeman said, "If there are social injustices, that's society's bag. We can't cure them; all we can do is make arrests."[29] Being a policeman was a hard job to begin with, but in the '60s, it was harder. Besides criminals, the police had to deal with political protests, and in Chicago, with larger gangs *and* a one-party system that could dictate much more policy to them than if there had been a viable two-party system. The Republicans had abdicated the running of Chicago politics to the Democrats and remained in control of the economic system. Informally, they'd given up on democracy in favor of a division of the spoils and, consequently, as one-party as Warsaw were Chicago politics. There was no one for the police to answer to except the Democrats. They'd deal with civil disorder through the police. Some of the choices were, of course, made for them by the government of the United States. The decisions were made that protected the justice system and all its abuses and put more technical power in the hands of urban police departments. Meanwhile, the city government moved to increase the size of the department by at least 700. According to the mayor's right-hand man, alderman Thomas Keane, Chicago needed more police to deal with the likes of Dr. Martin Luther King, Jr., who was—although non-violent himself—a front for violence.[30]

We can logically assume that the people who would take these new jobs in these times of strong anti-establishment sentiment from liberals and the more radical left were people not very much in agreement with the movement or in sympathy with ghetto residents in general. Attitude surveys of police taken in the late Sixties bear this out. In their opinions, the ghetto was created by the people that lived there, and, despite evidence to the contrary, they saw the movement, as J. Edgar Hoover saw it, as communist-inspired. In short, they felt black people lived in overcrowded, dirty conditions by choice and, if they were activists, they were probably communists (equated with anti-American).[31] Careful selection of officers and intensive training were needed for police recruits, but increased unrest hurried their training and lowered the standards for recruiting. Concurrently, the idea of one-man squad cars was implemented to increase the amount of coverage the police could give. It also increased the danger of the job.

The Chicago Police Department also jealously protected its officers and its right to remain independent of civilian control of any kind, particularly reviews of police actions; though a few police had killed innocent people, it was evidently felt that it was better they get away with it than allow civilian reviews that could stick. And so the elements for disaster were all present. And, anyone who owns a gun might stop to consider how easily it can interfere with a person's rationality if that person is in constantly dangerous environments with a license to use it at will. It is not implausible to assume that he or she might learn to reach for it habitually as a problem solver, particularly around people he doesn't like. And, a trait of midwestern Americans is they don't like people who don't look or act like them.

There was a white patrolman on the police force in the Sixties who patrolled Lawndale and was a member of the Ku Klux Klan by his own admission. Rumor was that he carried a nightstick, hollowed out, with a lead pipe shoved up inside, and that he'd been "punished" for beating a white kid senseless with it by being assigned to the black West Side at the Fillmore District Station. Apparently, this was normal procedure. So, although the volatile ghetto needed the better police, it got more of the brutal type than other communities. What distinguishes this patrolman from 50 other Ku Kluxers in the department (according to the Klan itself) is that his membership was "discovered," and he and five others were expelled from the department.[32]

The remaining forty-four Klansmen were evidently there in April 1968 when the riot following Dr. King's assassination occurred. The police, however, did a creditable job according to the experts, used a minimum of deadly force, and were praised for their restraint and regard for lives. Mayor Daley, on the other hand, was displeased with them and issued his much-publicized "shoot to kill arsonists, shoot to maim looters!" orders. And soon afterward, Chicago police began to patrol the black communities armed with loaded shotguns. The consequences of the Mayor's attitude and resulting actions were, according to independent investigators, "unmistakable and irrevocable." He unleashed the more violent on the force. The 1968 Democratic convention followed, and restraint was in the wind. As radicals, liberals, and passersby were getting their heads beat in the streets of downtown Chicago, the Illinois Black Panther Party was forming only a couple of miles away. Their battle cry, "Off the Pigs!" would strike both a bitter hatred from police and a responsive chord from liberals.

The spring of 1969 began where the violence of the summer of '68 ended. On May 1, 1969, Charles Cox, black, age 20, was found dead in a cell at the Fillmore District Station. A private pathologist testified in court that Cox died from blows to his head. Cox, of 3924 W. Monroe, had been arrested the night before. He and his friend were either causing a disturbance or walking down the street, disturbing no one (depending on who you believe) when the police picked them up. Cox was held, and his friend was let go. He returned with more friends, insisting Cox be let go. He was told Cox wasn't there, yet he heard his friend's voice. Cox definitely was there, and the next morning, his body was prepared for burial. The police listed drug overdose as the cause of death, but the skull evidenced a severe beating.[33]

One week later, May 8th, another killing by police was making news. This time, the victim was 35-year-old M.C. Green of 1922 Trumball. And yet another complaint came in on the same day to State Senator Charles Chew, from a youth beaten by a white mob, taken by the police and beaten again.[34]

On May 13, a West Side rally protested the killing of another teen, 17-year-old James Johnson. Johnson and his friends had run a red light and sped away with the police in pursuit. Their car hit a post. The police caught them and, according to eyewitnesses, shot him dead without provocation.[35]

In July, one night, 19-year-old Linda Anderson got in an argument with a friend. Linda was evidently struggling with him in her apartment when a rookie policeman came to her door. He demanded entrance, he later said. She yelled for him to go away. He went back to his squad car, got his new shotgun, returned, and blew a hole in the door—to force his way in, he said. The shot missed the lock he claimed he was shooting at, missed it by a foot or more, and plowed through the door, struck and killed the young woman.

The neighbors claimed he went to the door without knocking, shot at the woman's voice, blowing her brains out. Two facts were at odds with his version: that he missed the lock by so much and that the door was plywood, and he could have kicked it in. The fact that the neighbors believed it was murder indicates, moreover, what they thought the police were like. But whichever way it happened, Linda was dead from a case of gun mentality, and the officer received a one-day suspension for violating General Order 67-14, firing through a closed door.[36]

The next day the Panthers marched on the Fillmore District Police Station; lining up on the street across from the station, they shouted, "Death to oppressors, off the pigs!" Weeks later, young Panther Larry Roberson told two Fillmore District officers involved in questioning a man about a robbery that he would not move on—that it was his right to witness an arrest. An altercation followed, and Larry was shot in the stomach by the police. Apparently, on the road to recovery, he was taken from a private hospital to the Bridewell facility at Cook County Jail. There, in the Jail's custody, he mysteriously died. To the Panthers, it was an obvious sign of escalation from the police—they were not above murdering anyone anyway they saw fit, was the message.

In early August 1969, a South Side boy, Wayne Black, was killed by a policeman. The policeman claimed Wayne lunged at him with a knife. Three eyewitnesses denied it. The officer went free.[37]

On August 12, Maple Shorten, a 42-year-old man in good health—until the police arrested him for suspicioned drug pedaling. On August 13th, his wife went out to 26th and California (Criminal Courts) to hear his case. She was told, "Didn't you know he is dead already?"[38] There were 39 deaths in Chicago that year from the barrel of a policeman's gun.

The Panthers and the Young Lords marched on the Bridgeport police station, held public hearings, and mock trials that indicated the evidence of police misconduct, and threatened. Not a single case went to court or even brought back an indictment. Over on the South Side, the first overt response from black youth came with the killing of a black policeman who had threatened them. They were Stones, and he'd told them he'd kill six of them a week if he was in Stone territory. Evidently, they believed him.

**Black police respond.** A new organization, the Afro-American Patrolmen's League, protested the rising brutality of their fellow officers. They were a segment of the police in the department who viewed the situation as blacks and as police, with growing alarm. There was a war sentiment beginning to run through the police department and through black youth. This was a war with black police in the middle. A few black police began to react to the sentiments.

Bobby Rush, Deputy Minister of Defense of the Party, stepped up to the microphone in the People's Church on Ashland Avenue. "Will the 'Pigs' please leave? We ain't talking about nothin' until you do!" The two members of the Police Gang Intelligence looked at each other and at those around them. They were the only clean-cut, 35-40-year-olds in the group. Night after night, they were assigned just to sit there silently and identify those who came. They shrugged, looked at each other again. Their eyes said, "We've done our job." They got up and left.

"This is intelligence work?" Officer Howard Saffold asked. "This is bullshit. They're not giving us intelligence work!" His partner answered, "Damned right." Back at headquarters, they wrote out their nightly report: thirteen known Panthers attended such and such a meeting. Panther Brown wore usual leather jacket; Stephanie had usual red scarf sticking out of her coat pocket. Rush carried usual satchel, as he is known to do...

Officer O'Bannon approached them, 'We're gun to raid da Pant'ers tomorrah mornin'," he said. At the briefing that morning, 200 patrolmen were assembled. The artillery and equipment were handed out; an officer read, "Officer Cizewski will carry a shotgun and .357 Magnum, Officer Jones carries a .38 and a high-beam flashlight, etc. They joked about how the white boys got the heavy stuff.

The plan was to tail the volunteer community worker that rode the

Madison Street bus every morning to the Panthers' office. Once she got the door unbolted, they were to bust in and catch a fugitive. It was the head guy's big chance. The mood of the police was hot and heavy. "Boy, I'd love to blow one of those fuckers' heads off. Just one shot from any of them, and I'm killing a motherfucker today," one officer said, and got in reply several, "fuckin' A's!"

They hated the Panther Party for treating them with disrespect, the same kind of disrespect the police seemingly dished out on Afro-Americans by allowing police killers to go free. They could have, as professionals, ignored the Panther's attitudes and done their job, or they could take it as a challenge to their own macho image. Generally speaking, they did the latter. Meanwhile, young folks enjoyed the Panther attitude and enjoyed police anger. They didn't automatically respect a person because he wore a uniform and carried a gun, and they loved to challenge authority, particularly arrogant authority.

Black police officers like Howard Saffold and Buzz Palmer began to feel uneasy around the sentiment of their fellow officers. To them, Panthers were no worse than Nazis who talked about killing off Jews and black people. In fact, the Panthers were more understandable, seen as victims of oppression. If they could tolerate those Nazis, they could tolerate anyone.

One officer had grown up with a guy who was a Panther. The guy had bad-mouthed him, but he could see it was all rhetoric, with little personal feeling behind it.

The police, generally, weren't so tolerant. In this instance, they burst into the Panther headquarters angry, and when the raid was over and the place secured, and one policeman hurt, they burned the building, tore out the wiring, and beat the Panthers with their guns. It was then that Officer Saffold asked to be transferred. "Sure, we don't want you if you don't want to be here," they told him.[39] It seemed they hadn't wanted him there anyway, so they could carry on their personal war. The police department had given him a nasty job as an overt spy, a front for intimidating the Panthers in full view of them. Now, when his morale dipped, he got no encouragement; instead, he got a little push out the door.

Meanwhile, Saffold had gained a certain respect for the Panthers. Unlike gang-bangers, they didn't break down under police interrogation. They didn't seem to feel anyone was better than them, that they'd been caught doing something wrong. Police disrespect didn't intimidate them;

it made them angry. "The Panthers," claimed one paranoid police officer, "have invaded the police force."[40] This was, probably, in response to the obvious respect the Panthers got from black police officers. It seemed the police department refused to recognize the racism in its own ranks and its effects on black officers. Racism was so rampant that the intelligence program, which necessarily relied on black police officers where the Panthers were concerned, was crippled because the white leader of the Gang Intelligence Unit was refusing to relay the information he got to his black co-leader."[41]

The police violence of that year, 1969, has been documented. And although few police ever kill anyone, and most probably never brutalize; nevertheless, the Chicago Police were, by far, the most trigger-happy big-city police across the country that year. Something was obviously out of hand, and what was happening and how it would be resolved was totally ignored by the Chicago news media. Here are the statistics that, to this day, are unanswered as to why:

## CHICAGO VICTIMS OF POLICE USE OF FATAL FORCE[15]

|  | 1969 | 1970 | 1969-70 |
|---|---|---|---|
| Black people killed | 27 | 32 | 59 (3 female) |
| White people killed | 13 | 6 | 19* (no female) |

* Four of white victims were Latino; one other victim unidentified.

## COMPARISON WITH OTHER CITIES — 1970

| City | Population | Citizens Killed | Ratio to Population |
|---|---|---|---|
| New York | 7.86 million | 21 | 0.27 |
| Chicago | 3.36 million | 32 | 0.95 |
| Los Angeles | 2.82 million | 8 | 0.28 |
| Philadelphia | 1.95 million | 13 | 0.67 |
| Detroit | 1.51 million | 4 | 0.26 |

## OTHER INTERESTING STATISTICS

- In the years 1969 and 1970, 79 Chicago civilians were killed by the police.
- Fifty-eight times, the police claimed the victim they killed had a weapon; three out of the 58 times was a weapon produced.
- Twenty-eight of the 79 killings gave clear indication of police misconduct.
- No police were brought to court; only one case reached the grand jury level.

One possible answer is that the Chicago Police Department was the one institution that a citizen could join to kill black people. Given the political climate and the heightened racial tensions in Chicago, perhaps people had done just that. The fact that the Chicago police were killing people at a rate three times that of any of the country's large cities except Philadelphia leads to the conclusion that a racist organization was inside the department, carrying out its own policy, which included —or at least did not exclude—murder.

What would happen in the coming fall of 1969 was the direct result of these facts that summer (1) a few police were killing young Afro-Americans and getting off, and (2) the locally admired Panthers were in the streets, in the midst of this police violence, shouting "Off the pigs!" Something had to happen.

# Chapter 5

# ISOLATION OF THE PARTY

**Panthers and the Police.** The phone rang at the new Panther headquarters on Madison. Several Party members quit talking so that Deputy Chairman Fred could hear. "This is the Chicago Police Department. We've just been over to SDS to beat their door down. You Cocksuckers are next!" Fred replied, "Come on!" Police harassment had just begun. By spring 1969, the police had made ninety-five arrests of known Party members.[42] The pattern of harassment was to arrest them for anything, release them when bail was posted, then drop the charges. A typical period is illustrated in the accompanying chart.[43]

| Date | Name | Charge |
|---|---|---|
| April 1, 1969 | Jackie Robinson | disorderly conduct |
| April 1 | Lance Bell, Randle Rollins, Michael McCarty | disorderly conduct |
| April 2 | Jewell Cook | illegally parked car |
| April 12 | Marcus Jones | theft (of garbage can) |
| April 17 | Freddie Robinson | burglary |
| May 1 | Garry Taylor | no tail lights (after police car rammed into his) |
| May 1 | J. Robinson, Rollins, Lance Bell | disorderly conduct |

The Party didn't have enough money to handle the bail and legal counsel; they were going broke. Party members were quitting under the strain. Those who stayed with it began harassing the police with insults while they continued to work at organizing the teenagers of Chicago. The police started visiting the free breakfast programs, trying to scare the children away by taking photos of them. They picked up community volunteers "for questioning" and dropped them off across town. As spring turned to summer, patience was wearing thin with the police. They weren't stopping the programs, but they were angering the community; now things got rougher. The Panthers were hurting but not crippled. The FBI took the lead.

The FBI had failed in its first attempt to disrupt the Party—by turning the Rangers on them, and now the Illinois Panther Party was perhaps the strongest in the nation, outside of Oakland. So, the FBI tried the direct approach, and it worked. On June 4th at 5:35 a.m., they raided Panther headquarters, using bullhorns and tear gas, and armed with submachine guns and a helicopter. The eight Panthers inside the headquarters surrendered quietly. They were impressed with the FBI and with the technology. The raiders arrested all eight and charged them with harboring an unfound fugitive. They took from the Party $3,000 in donations, a list of donors, a list of members, food for the free breakfast program, and six legally purchased weapons—and never gave them back. The excuse for the raid was their supposed search for "fugitive" George Sams, who, in reality, was an informant of theirs.[44] In fact, informant O'Neal (in daily contact with them) had probably told the FBI that Sams wasn't there.

Marlin Johnson, head of the Chicago FBI office (who now heads the review board on police brutality cases), led this raid personally.[45] Johnson and his office are, to this day, unconvicted burglars. But the FBI had accomplished what it probably set out to do. It made a majority of the Panther community workers reconsider working for the Party. The size of community participation in the Party's programs never again equaled what it had before that raid.[46] Black people were not willing to challenge the FBI or to try overthrowing the government. On the other hand, there was Chicago's establishment and its police.

The very next day, police intimidation was characteristically more clumsy. They arrested eleven Party members on the South Side; one was pregnant. She was kicked and suffered a bleeding kidney. This undisguised brutality brought a response of increased animosity from the youth of the community. The more racist of the police kept pushing the Panthers. Perhaps they felt they could get these "boys" to play the "nigger" role.

The average citizens, those who felt they couldn't actively support the Black Panther Party as philosophy, were nevertheless antagonized by police brutalizing black people and seemingly getting away with it. To the police, it may have looked as if black society was jeopardizing their lives to the criminals by the rising cry of, "Off the pigs!" They had, however, earned the response they got by protecting the brutal, even murderous policemen in their ranks and by opposing any disorder by black people— criminal activity or civil disobedience. The police, the white police, and some blacks, closed ranks on their critics and assumed a war mentality. "We're gunnta win the war with you people!" the officer told the young black woman as he wrote her a traffic ticket, according to the Chicago Defender. "What war's that?" she asked.

The patrolman's point of view was that any attack on brutality hit their most sensitive nerve and means of control. How to keep a lid on a rebellious ghetto seemingly was the ghetto policeman's primary job, not primarily preserving the law. The legal system was so tangled and so rampant with loopholes, legal and illegal, it was probably impossible to serve the law and serve society. Criminals, non-political criminals, that is, could be on the streets soon after they were arrested. Fear, the police evidently figured, kept the lid on. Mayor Daley himself identified the policeman's job: ". . . the policeman isn't there to create disorder, the policeman was there to preserve disorder."[47] Although Daley meant to say order, the "preserve" part was on target—preserving the status quo.

Society puts the pressure on people who don't play the "proper" role. Poor people are supposed to take society's disrespect, it seems, then take it out on someone else or release it through drugs, liquor, getting the "holy ghost." The release makes life less agitating, less angry. Panthers refused the role and the releases. After months of police abuse, they were in a pent-up rage. A rage that would last among them for years. In a society in which everyone takes a little "shit" and where poor people, particularly poor black people, generally take the most, the Panthers said, "We ain't taking no more shit!"

In a society in which man is not allowed to be a man, in the old-time sense of the word, in the sense that Crazy Horse or Hudie Ledbetter was a man—a man so consumed by his love of life and the living of it, that he would live it out his way, though it led to an early death, that macho spirit cried out for that romantic manhood. Among the young, the tough, the spirit of manhood rose up against injustice in that old way. Yet if romanticism is beautiful, it also tends to be reckless, even arrogant. Good politics and romanticism are sometimes antagonistic. To paraphrase Mao: Heroism leads to conceit, conceit produces dogmatism, dogmatism alienates the people.

Internal developments hurt the Party that summer. Stokely Carmichael quit the Party, calling it "dishonest" and criticizing its alliances with (and seeming philosophical dominance by) white radicals. In Oakland, the Party's direction was undergoing changes. Continuous policy changes from Oakland, specifically the endorsing of gay liberation and the forced reading of Mao, rubbed a lot of Chicago Panthers wrong. They generally felt they didn't need Mao to tell them what time it was, and they didn't approve of "sissies." Homosexuality was, from their experiences, another cop-out for black men, a way to avoid the responsibilities of manhood. In fact, at the very moment Huey Newton was making the announcement in support of gay liberation at the Party's convention in Philadelphia, a group of Chicago Panthers was launching an attack on the "gays" who had invaded the auditorium to boo the "male chauvinist Panthers."[48] Huey may have turned the "gay" boos to cheers, but he also turned the Panther determination into confusion. What was the purpose of the Illinois Black Panther Party? Were they community liberators who believed in socialism, or were they the vanguard party of a nationwide (or worldwide) Marxist coalition? Fred accepted the changes as they came from Oakland, but many equally dedicated Panthers could not. Experienced leaders were leaving the Party as a result; leaders who had challenged Fred had intellectually stimulated him and subjected his ideas to analysis. Decisions were beginning to fall consistently on 20-year-old Chairman Fred and no one else. Bob Brown was gone; most of SNCC was gone.

The people that hung with Fred hung because they were fighters, people of the community where the Party existed. Fred was the best leader they'd seen. They had faith in him as a fighter, and they had the strength of their own fighting tradition. For them, the Panthers were not revolutionary in the sense of being a new role-breaking phenomenon. As much as they joined the Party, the Party had joined them; it had given structure to their attitudes. It was a set of attitudes the old folks understood. Fighting for liberation was nothing they felt they needed to analyze. It was their Southern tradition. All they wanted was Fred's leadership. If he were a Marxist, okay, they were. With most experienced leaders gone, the Party now really needed its Chairman. And on May 26th, Chairman Fred went to jail, convicted of stealing that same old ice cream in Maywood. So the Panthers faced that summer without the one leader left who was politically astute.

The first major collision between the police and the leaderless Party occurred at Panther headquarters on July 31st. Here is how the raid of July 31, 1969, happened at Panther headquarters:

The dark blue squad car with a white roof cruised down busy Madison Avenue in the heart of Mile Square. It caught the sunlight as it emerged from the shadow of the elevated tracks near the Chicago Stadium, heading west in the warm, sunny afternoon. The white police wore dark "shades" and stuck out in the busy Afro-American environment. As they approached the light at Oakley Boulevard, they got a few stares and returned them in kind until the people looked away. They drove more slowly as they approached the two-story, gray cement and granite building on the right side of the street, Panther headquarters. One officer glanced at the door of the headquarters, then began his stare, met by more than a returning stare. From the door, a big fellow leaned toward them, shouting, "Yeah, we here motherfuckers!" The challenge rang in the warm air, stilling the street talk and echoing in the minds of the people. An old woman on the corner looked to be thinking, "What is this young man trying to do, get himself killed?" People tensed up, some with pride, others with fear. They knew how violent the police could be; after all, Linda Anderson, Charles Cos, and Larry Roberson had just recently been killed. So it was smart to be cool. But the Panthers were past educating and past being cool; they wanted a fight.

The police went around the block and came back with four more squad cars. They were evidently going to demand respect for the badge by any means necessary. Their rage had also reached a high. They were ready to openly disrespect the law to get the "respect" (or servility) they wanted.

The five squad cars parked across the street from Panther head-quarters and began to question (according to the police) or harass (according to Panthers) a couple of young people, Panthers actually, in a car, daring the rest of the Panthers on the north side of Madison to interfere. The Panthers formed a marching line on their side of the street, shouting on cue, "Pigs, oink-oink, oink-oink!" The scene had all the appearances of a pre-war ritual. And evidently no one was there to stop it and remind some of the participants that these police might be the unthinking tools of bigger bosses. Late that night, the police returned.

The police had been going through mock raids for weeks, running to the door of the Panther office with guns drawn. The Panthers had taken to walking the alleys with guns, daring passing police cars to stop. This time, as one officer pulled his pistol, he was fired on from the office. He returned the fire. The shots echoed in the deserted, dirty, paper-filled street. A Panther who was coming out the door raced down the street. Old, dark, handsome "Lucky" (a lady's man in his younger days), one of the few old-timers in the Panther Party, raced for help. The policeman fired again at the second-floor window where the shots came from, then reached back into his squad car for his shotgun. The crack of a pistol shot from Panther headquarters rang out, and the officer was shot in the leg and limped behind his car. The police radioed for help and, suddenly, the community of Mile Square was alive with sirens and gunfire. They heard it in the projects up on Washington and the row houses on Monroe. People began to come up on Madison to find out what was happening. "The pigs are [finally] vampin'!"

It had become a full-scale battle. The police evidently felt the Panthers weren't serious at first and carelessly exposed themselves. They were serious. In ten or fifteen minutes, five or six officers were wounded. The gunfire on the office was heavy, but it had been equipped for such a raid with sandbags and lead shields. The Panthers had the tactical advantage. A crowd gathered as the fight continued. About 300 people were enthusiastically watching but clearly not participating in a Panther class in tactics that became a police class in revenge when the Panthers inside ran out of ammunition and surrendered. As they came down the stairs, they were grabbed by the police. The first one caught a rifle butt in his jaw, breaking it. The next one got a barrel jammed in his throat. They were beaten, kicked, pulled to their feet, and taken back inside, where the police fired shots over their heads into the walls. Then the police brought a couple gallons of gasoline and doused the walls of the second floor, they ripped out the improvised wiring (put in after the FBI's raid), took $500 in donations and some food, and set the place on fire.[49] The Panthers were thrown into a paddy wagon while three police charged into the rapidly angering crowd, grabbed another youth too bold with his insults, and shoved him into the wagon also. Bottles and rocks rained on the police and their squad cars. Through this storm, the paddy wagon pulled off with its load of Panthers and one spectator. When they reached the Wood Street station, they were forced to run a gauntlet of billy clubs. Amidst the beating, the smallest one continuously shouted—almost joyous at the severity of the beating—he concluded, "We mustaoffed a pig! We mustaoffed a pig!"[50] He was ecstatic.

Back at Panther headquarters, the neighbors had become aroused. These were their friends. They were on the verge of starting a riot. "Let's get our guns and have it out with them!" And they began to bust windows and loot stores to draw the police back. But Panther Bobby Rush was going through the crowd, cooling people off. "Cool it," he said, "We ain't ready for this." They slowly broke up.[51] The next day, the people of the community began to help the Panthers repair their office.

If members had been popular before with young folks, they were a phenomenon after the police-Panther battles. This was the kind of courage young people understood easiest. The Panthers hadn't acted crazy, hadn't attacked a police station, they'd just not backed off—they had fought! They were heroes! And, as much as the young admired it, the older folks shuddered, began pulling their kids away if possible. Association with the Panther Party was surely a most dangerous thing.

It was also, despite their professing Marxism, seemingly un-Marxist to make the working class police their most significant enemy. They were angry warriors up against angry police; Marxism, on the other hand, was/is coldly scientific, the science of revolution. What they expressed was a love for their people, an anger at disrespect, and not much science or politics to it.

**The split in the youth movement.** The youthful end of the civil rights movement as it moved from social rights (where black people could sit on a bus, etc.) to economics, had moved toward political revolution, on that there was agreement. In the post-World War years to 1968, the movement had also changed from an integration movement to a black power movement—the idea of gaining power. How to go about this revolution of power and how far to go was unclear. But black pride, which was on the rise, seemed to be the heart of the disagreement. At first, blackness was emphasized, beginning with wearing your natural hair (naturals, they were called), being yourself, recognizing the African in the Afro-American. This exploded into dashiki-wearing, learning Swahili, imitating African cultures, and rejecting the American in the Afro-American. Young people were inclining toward a Pan-African movement, an international alliance of black people with anti-white overtones.

In the midst of this trend, the most publicized Afro-American organization, the Black Panther Party, rejected Pan-Africanism and African culture and advocated alliances with poor whites as a class union, crossing racial and cultural lines, and proclaiming the unity of all oppressed peoples. The Party said black solidarity was necessary among Afro-Americans, but emphasizing African culture was dysfunctional. They also said violent political revolution was the only solution. And in July 1969, Stokely Carmichael and the SNCC contingent quit the Party, calling it "dishonest" and criticizing its white alliances, claiming white influence had become too strong of a factor.

The issue that split the movement, therefore, was two-fold: not only was there a racial angle, but also, philosophically. Stokely did not want black people welded to a revolutionary Marxist analysis. Criticism of the Party by a good portion of what had been a unified youth movement was, after the July split, strong. To Fred Hampton, it was African culturalism (and racial animosities) carried to extremes. For him, and those who stayed with the Party, Marxism was not racial; it was an analysis that transcended race. As for Pan-African culture? Here's his reply:

> • We're talkin' about destroying the system, and they have
> hang-ups doing that because they're constantly buying
> property within that system. And it's kind of hard to burn up
> on Tuesday what you bought last Monday

> Objective reality. That's what the Black Panther Party deals
> with. We're not metaphysics, we're not idealists, we're
> dialectical materialists. And we deal with what reality is,
> whether we like it or not.

> A lot of people can't relate to that because everything they
> do is gaged by the way they like things to be. We say that's
> incorrect. You look and see how things are, and then you deal
> with that. We runnin' around talking about "we gonna love
> all black people. We have an undying love for black people."
> And you know what? That if Malcolm came back, he'd walk
> past a million Klansmen to get to Stokely and whoop his
> motherfuckin' ass. Because Malcolm [when he was killed]
> was standing right like this in a room where white people
> weren't even allowed. You hear me? They wouldn't allow
> no white people in there. But Malcolm's dead. Now, what
> happened?

• Because they had names with 37X, 15X, blacker than black, and they were able to sneak in because of this ignorant potient #9 that these maniacs are trying to whoop on us—"We gonna love all black people because every Negro is a potential black man."

The man testified against Chairman Bobby in the Conspiracy Trial down in Chicago was a black man. The man that has Chairman Bobby on a murder trial in Connecticut is a black man. The man who murdered Malcolm X is a black man. The judge that denied Eldridge Cleaver bond after a white man had granted him bond... was a black man.

• You heard about the conspiracy trial on the West Side that they were able to win, with Doug Andrews and Fats Crawford, when they had the big burn on the West Side in the Martin Luther King riot? Ask 'em! Brothers, what's wrong with you, brothers and sisters? Ask 'em was that a white man. No! Because Doug and them, they criticized us for our liberal stand. They call it liberal. So they don't let nobody in their 'hood but black people. But they didn't know. Anybody ever hear about Gloves [Davis] on the South Side of Chicago? He's not white. Did you think Buckney [head of Gang Intelligence, Chicago Police] was white? You think Buckney's white? Buckney, who's taking all of your brothers and all of your little sisters and all of your little cousins and nephews, and he's gonna continue to take 'em.

• We don't care if niggers wear dashikis. You understand? That's not gonna mean anything in the final analysis.

[On African Culture]

• You think we scared of a few karangatangs, a few chumps, a few male chauvinists? They tell their women, "Walk behind me." The only reason a woman should walk behind a faggot like that is so she can put her foot knee deep in his ass.

We don't need no culture except a revolutionary culture. What we mean by that is a culture that will free you. You heard our field lieutenant talking about a fire in the room, didn't you? What you worried about when you got a fire in this room? You worry about water or escape. You don't worry about nothin' else. If you say, "What's your culture during this fire?" "Water, that's my culture, brother, that's my culture." Because culture's a thing that keeps you. "What's your politics?" Escape and water.

• They say nigger, you ain't got no natural. Nigger, how come your name ain't changed? Huey P. Newton is named after a demagogic, lyin' politician, Huey P. Long?" And pigs don't care about that. Because you don't have to call, if your shotgun's a Browning, you don't have to give it no African name it shoots the same. You understand?

• Changin' your name is not gonna change our set of arrangements. The only thing that's gonna change our set of arrangements is what gotten us into this set of arrangements. And that's our oppressor. And it's on three stages, we call it three in one: avaricious, greedy businessmen, lying politicians, pig fascist, reactionary cops. Until you deal with those three things, then your set of arrangements will remain the same. The only difference will be that you'll still be under fascism, but instead of Fred being under fascism, I'll be Oogabooga under fascism. But I'll feel the same.[52]

Fred made sense, but his message wasn't reaching a very wide audience in Chicago. For why, a brief look must be taken at the media.

**The role of the media in isolating the Party.** The media, through its emphasis on violence, had already perverted the Alabama-born Panther movement. Now, through rumor-spreading, distortions, and many of the classical techniques of propoganda isolated the Panther Party from potential allies. And in fact, its sensationalism probably attracted young folks more into fantasizing as bad dudes. Media reporting was blatantly poor in research and prejudiced. The reasons are related to all the other factors in a racist society acting in fear of the Panther Party. The FBI, for example, admitted it fed stories to its friends in the press.

An example of this is the *Sun-Times* treatment of the FBI raid on Panther Party headquarters on June 4, 1969. Art Petacque's story was nothing less than the FBI's story. They raided the office, they said, looking for a fugitive, George Sams. Sams, it later turned out, was evidently an informant of theirs and was not there—as O'Neal had probably related to the FBI. What they found were photos of him, taken there in the Party's headquarters. The reporter's story also tells us they recovered a cache of weapons.[53] Now, you would think a trained reporter would ask why the Panthers were taking pictures of him in their headquarters. He didn't. Secondly, the word "recovered" implied that the guns were stolen; the word "cache" supposes they were hidden. The guns were all legally purchased, yet they, and several thousand dollars and a list of volunteers, were all stolen from the Party by the FBI. None of this made the *Sun-Times* story. What is obvious is that the reporter was not interested in the truth; he was only interested in the FBI's story. He would repeat this loose use of the truth three years later when covering the De Mau Mau.[54]

*The New Yorker* magazine, in an article on February 13, 1971, was more sophisticated but had similar head problems. The story quoted both Julian Bond and Ralph Abernathy as asserting that the leadership of the Black Panther Party was being destroyed by the federal government. The Panthers' attorney said 28 Panthers had been killed by the government. *The New Yorker's* reporter successfully refuted the exact number of Panthers killed. But having discredited the attorney, he feels he's discredited the entire assertion! He failed to ask Abernathy or Bond about their sources. What evidence did they have? How about those that were killed? Nothing said. This kind of reporting was a consistent problem.

Biases are not always purposely misleading, but distortion and propaganda are. Take the following example from the *Chicago Sun-Times*, April 3, 1969:

> A Black Panther plot to bomb five Manhattan department
> stores on Thursday during the Easter shopping rush has been
> broken up by indictment of 21 members of the militant Negro
> group, District Attorney Frank S. Hogan said Wednesday.

The early prominence of the words "Black Panther" and the
tardiness in which this paragraph is identified as a quote from the D.A.
is classic propaganda. Every journalism major knows that a story is
written to contain all pertinent information in the first few lines, based
on the assumption that that is all the reader sees. The average reader
wouldn't even catch the fact that this story is not fact but a rumor from
prosecutors, in a "plot" that did not exist. It also makes the Panther Party
out to be murderers caught just before the act of a senseless crime.

The Panther Free Breakfast for Children program began in April of
'69 and spread across the state, feeding black and white kids, thousands a
day. It never made the news media. Yet on June 11 of '69, in a prominent
sub-head, the *Sun-Times* carried a story that the Illinois legislature had
okayed (not begun) free lunches for kids.[55]

Are the Panthers violent people? The press relies on Cook County
State's Attorney Ed Hanrahan. Yes, because they've bought $8,000 worth
of guns in two years.[56] But if you think about it, that's not very many
guns. Say 50-60 guns, or 100 pistols, for an organization averaging about
100-200 people—minus the $2,000 worth of guns the FBI stole from
them. Compared to the Stones, they are unarmed; compared to the Klan?
The Nazis? Compared to the amount of money they've spent on free
lunches for kids, free medical services for Lawndale? No one checked.
From the *Sun-Times*:

> "Fred Hampton was familiar to the police.... He had been
> charged more than a half-dozen times with mob action,
> aggravated battery, and disorderly conduct as he angrily
> pressed the militant program of the Black Panther Party."[57]

This paragraph involved nothing but misleading statements. First is
guilt by association. Being charged over a half-dozen times (what is that,
seven times, eight?) implies guilt, yet all those charges had been dropped
because they were trumped-up charges. Further, the mob action charge
had been a standard weapon of the Democratic Machine against rioters in
the previous year because it provided for up to a year in prison,  though
it was a misdemeanor (and it was probably unconstitutional). It was also
accompanied by bail ten times higher than normal, which violated an
Illinois statute requiring that misdemeanor bonds be no more than double
the maximum fine.[58]

*The Daily News* reported that Donald Berry, a member of the Detroit Panther Party (a chapter at times controlled by the FBI), said the killing of a Chicago policeman in August 1970, probably by a Stone, was part of a nationwide Panther program. In no way could the Panther Party be linked to this murder, yet the paper printed the rumor. Chicago police told reporters, following a shooting incident, that the Panther involved had papers identifying him with the "mysterious section two committee" of the Panther Party. Pure fiction, but reporters passed it on to the readers.[59]

*The Chicago Defender* did some fine reporting on police brutality in 1969, but ignored the existence of an Illinois Black Panther Party. So, while the white press emphasized the violence between police and Panthers and ignored police violence on other citizens, the *Defender* reported the violence of the police on non-Party citizens. Reading them both you get the picture that, in the same way, the police action against the Panthers was escalating, their attitude toward citizens was escalating.

Along with the distortions were a few good reporting jobs. On May 25, 1969, for example, *Sun-Times* reporter William Braden interviewed Fred Hampton and gave a good account of the Panthers' program. It was, however, placed right under a story about Hanrahan's war on gangs, thus associating gangs and the Party.

Generally, the image of the Panthers was portrayed as irrational. A large part of the news was derived from policy by inexperienced or biased reporters. The press ignored analyses and related stories that might have shed light on the Illinois Black Panther Party, the Mile Square situation, or the police. The resignation of Lu Palmer, a black journalist for the *Chicago Daily News*, is significant. When he asked to report on the community service programs of the Black Panther Party, they told him the paper had to protect its public from certain realities.

The media was a part of the isolation of the Black Panther Party from black Chicago readers who were not adept enough at detecting the subtle distortions and half-truths that made good propaganda. The media's role and their failure to acknowledge it also indicate that any attempt at social change in the black community in the future will not get a fair hearing through the press. In fact, media attention might be a major problem of a grass roots movement, attracting by its misrepresentations, people who have the wrong idea concerning the goals of the movement.

The press in Chicago evidently doesn't mind ignoring whatever it wants to ignore, even when the omission wreaks havoc with common sense. As an example, a situation comparable to the Afro-American struggle in Chicago in 1968-80 is the so-called Catholic versus Protestant fight in Northern Ireland. The press reports the violence but never explains the whys. They report the sensational, but unless it is in their interest, they ignore the reasons. Who are the Irish Protestants, and what is this fight about? Is it over religious dogma, social programs, English oppression? Not a word of explanation do we get. Likewise, with the Panther Party right here at home, the violence is all we get. By irresponsibly reporting only violence, they fanned it, if only because the police rely on the press too, and that kind of tale would make any policeman's trigger finger itch.

Malcolm X explains:

> When I say they use the press, that doesn't mean that all reporters are bad. Some of them are good, I suppose. But you can take their collective approach to any problem and see that they can always agree when it gets to you and me. They knew that the Afro-American Broadcasting Company was giving this affair which is designed to honor outstanding black Americans, is it not? But you find nothing in the newspapers that gives the slightest hint that this affair was going to take place—not one hint, though there are supposed to be many sources for news. If you don't think that they're in cahoots, watch. They are all interested, or none of them is interested. . . . They're not going to say anything in advance about an affair that's being given by any black people who believe in functioning beyond the scope of the ground rules that are laid down by the liberal elements of the power structure.

> When you start thinking for yourselves, you frighten them, and they try and block your getting to the public, for they fear that if the public listens to you then the public won't listen to them anymore. And they've got certain Negroes whom they have to keep blowing up in the papers to make them look like leaders. So that the people will keep following them, no matter how many knocks they get on their heads following them. This

is how the man does it.[60]

By late summer 1969, the Party was forced to alter its stance on revolution. Repression had come so swiftly, and from so many directions (from local police, the FBI, local thugs, spies, politicians, and the media) that advocating revolution was not just reckless, it was becoming suicidal. In Chicago, confusion arose as to what the Party said it embodied and what it actually embodied. That summer, for example, the first overt change coming from Oakland policy changes was the formation of a splinter group; a group that was to challenge police repression within the system. And so, the National Committee to Combat Fascism (NCCF) was born. Across the nation, local Panther chapters sponsored their new sub-group.

The NCCF, an outgrowth of immediate massive violence against a group that preached revolution (the Panther Party), was designed to use the system to reform police institutions or at least buy time for the Party. However, the NCCF office, which opened in Chicago on 35th Street near Indiana Avenue, was a center for Afro-American nationalism. Like quite a few of the Party members, the teens who made up the NCCF learned how the police stop bullets, and that was what they talked. To them, revolution meant using guns to get the police off black youths.

Massive repression meant the Party suffered in its ability to establish rapport or to utilize the people attracted by elements of its message.

As the actions of the Panther Party seeped through press gossip-and-rumors people, some people began to realize that, while the Party talked revolution, its actions were generally positive. That and the idea that the establishment was wiping them out for preaching violence (while the Nazis went on with impunity preaching hatred and violence) made it evident that an injustice was taking place. The idea of that racist injustice brought me, at the time, a 22-year-old teacher who would otherwise have ignored them as some crazy militants, to Chicago's West Side. I remember driving off the Eisenhower Expressway at Western Avenue and heading north on Madison Street. I felt what I was doing was dangerous but necessary for my conscience's sake. I had recently heard about another police attack on Panther headquarters and wanted to give some support to people of whom I was, by habit, more frightened than the police. I parked on Western next to Mickie's hot dog stand, locked the car tight, and walked a few doors down the crowded, lively street to Panther headquarters. This was the heart of the ghetto in 1969, as crowded and noisy as Central and Madison is now. The first thing I noticed was the heavy metal door to the office, unhinged and propped up against the wall with several shotgun blasts in it.

I went to the door and rang the buzzer. From a loudspeaker overhead, a voice metallically shouted, "All power to the people, who is it!" Sounded like an army post in war, but I liked the "All power to the people." I shouted my name back. "What do you want!" the voice shouted back at me. People on the street watched this scene with amusement; I, in a white shirt and tie. I was embarrassed and ready to leave. Fortunately, another voice said, "Open the door, man." The door buzzed, and I went in. There were two young men behind a desk at the top of a long set of stairs, one tall, thin, and dark, the other short and stocky, built like a little tank, named Oppress. Oppress said, "Everything out your pockets and spread against the wall!" They patted me down, went through the wallet, and handed it back. They hadn't taken anything; I checked. "What do you want?" Oppress asked, friendly and businesslike. The other guy looked mean and stared. I said, "I came over to volunteer." I didn't feel it was the right time to say that I didn't agree with them totally, etc. The tall, lean guy took Oppress aside, and I realized they were arguing over whether I was a plainclothed police or a fool or what. I was having my own argument over whether the tall, thin one was a thug or a fool. "Okay," he finally said, "You got a 'short' [a car]? Okay, you can take me and these two youngbloods over to the new center on Pulaski and 16th."

We went out and got in my ride. "Say, man," he said, "you know the next time we have a riot, we are going to take it to the white neighborhoods, right youngbloods?" Thinking about what happened to black folks even rioting in their own neighborhoods, I had visions of two youngsters hanging from a tree. "Pull over here, bro," he said as I searched for a way out of this dude's power. "Right on!" the youngsters had responded to his crazy suggestion. It was enough for me for one day.

I went back the next weekend and the next, and so on. I got used to the shakedown and began to work regularly with them on weekends, driving them to speaking engagements, sharing meals, helping collect donations.

Once, I went into a sweat as a young Panther sister tried to cuss a policeman from the back seat of my car. I had let him in front of me at a traffic jam. You see, I had four sisters and 50 pounds of Panther papers with mean little drawings of police as pigs with flies buzzing around them and overloaded with guns and I wasn't about to give that police officer cause to look at me hard. So, the rest of the ride was a little tense between me and the sisters. In fact, that was it for me and them. They ignored me from then on whenever I came to the office and asked to help. I'd stand there, and they'd give me nothing to do. The memory that stands with me is one of mutual paranoia, a tragic memory, considering what was to follow.

Strangers had come up to me while I was working for them, catch me alone, and say, "You hear about that woman the Panthers killed in the alley behind their office?... They all a bunch of small-time thugs and pickpockets. Fred, he's a good man, now if he'd just stop that heavy gambling with Party funds!" These were all well-dressed, respectable people. I knew they were lying after the first time, and it simply opened my eyes to how heavily the Panthers were being attacked, undermined. Finally, I got a visit from the FBI. Who was I turning the donation money I got over to? My father got a similar visit, and questions like, was I the Rice from Peoria that robbed a grocery store there? Between the Panthers and the federal police, my experience was a case of bad politics on both of their parts. How are you ever going to win people over by hounding them or excluding them? The Party was not only being isolated, they were isolating themselves.

What had happened to the Lowndes County approach? What had happened to voter registration, winning the people no matter who they were? They were a clique now, courageous, formally anti-racist, but still a clique. They wanted guys who fit the tough image. (They'd have thrown out a West Point grad.) And, with all that was going on around them, they still talked of violent retaliation.

Summer was turning into early fall, and Fred was released from Menard prison in southern Illinois and returned to the Party. He was a little different Fred, they all said; more serious, maybe not as cocky. He had evidently been told in jail that his days were numbered, if not directly, by the jail experience itself. But their hopes were high with his return. His first day out, he spoke to an exuberant crowd of youths, black and white, armed to the teeth. Yes, things had changed in Chicago too; the name for the change was escalation, and for the Panther Party, isolation.

# Chapter 6

# THE CLIMACTIC EVENTS OF LATE 1969

**The Soto Brothers, October.** The adults of the local community were feeling like they had to be careful in dealing with the Panthers and were probably not as close as before. Life was tough, and staying alive and keeping their kids healthy was number one. Three violent raids on Panther headquarters that summer showed them how dangerous association with the Panther Party could be.

But there was an immediate concern that drew the Party and the adults to a common cause; it was the dangerous intersection at Washington and Hoyne Avenues in front of the Henry Horner Homes.

In September, two kids were killed crossing the street on that corner.

> It was Huey P. Newton who taught us how the people learn. You learn by participation. When Huey P. Newton started out, what did he do? He got a gun, and he got Bobby, and Bobby got a gun. They had a problem in the community because people were being run over—kids were being run over—at a certain intersection. What did the people do? The people went down to the government to redress their grievances, and the government told them to go to hell. "We are not going to put no stoplights down there UNTIL WE SEE FIT." What did Huey P. Newton do? Did he go out and tell the people about the laws, and write letters, and try to propagandize them all the time? No! Some of that is good, but the masses of the people don't read—that's what I heard Huey say—they learn through observation and participation. Did he just say this? No! So what did he do? He got him a shotgun, he got Bobby,

and he got him a hammer and went down to the corner. He
gave Bobby the shotgun and told him if any pig motherfucker
come by blow his motherfuckin' brains out. What did he do?
He went to the corner and nailed up a stop sign. No more
accidents, no more trouble. And then he went back —another
situation like that. What did the people do? They looked at
it, they observed, they didn't get a chance to participate in it.
Next time, what'd they do? Some kind of problem came up.
The PEOPLE got their shotguns, got their nine millimeters,
got their hammers. How'd they learn? They learned by
observation and participation... He led the people down the
correction road of revolution. What are we doing?

—Fred Hampton[61]

The situation at Hoyne and Washington was obviously parallel; in
fact, some Panthers say the situation Fred described in Oakland never
happened. Fred liked to teach and to teach by actions. And it was also
a means for the Party to reaffirm its stand with the community. When
the community petition for a stoplight was ignored, the Panther Party
took the lead. They stood in the street and stopped traffic, unarmed.
Fred's actions were most often more pragmatic and less dramatic than his
rhetoric.

The people of Henry Horner Projects imitated the Party, and massive
civil disobedience won for them a stoplight.[62] And to be sure, given the
climate between the community and the police, and particularly between
Panthers and the police, we can be sure the district police were most
unhappy with that show of clout. Two of the most identifiable people
involved in the protest activity were the half-Puerto Rican, half-black
Soto boys, Michael, 21, and John, 16. Tall, black-haired, light brown
complexion, they looked Puerto Rican rather than black. On Sunday
night, October 5th, around 10 p.m., John was shot and killed by a police
officer. The officer, John Nolan, claimed he killed young John Soto as
the boy leaped at him. Strangely, the boy was shot in the back of the
head. Witnesses said he shot the boy in cold blood, without provocation.
Witnesses could not agree on whether the bullet ricocheted and killed
the boy or whether it was direct and at close range. But from the stories
all pieced together, it is clear, and all versions are in agreement, that

patrolman Nolan had pulled his gun to stop two kids passing a bottle. If he had pulled his nightstick, John Soto would still be alive. Beyond that, the circumstances with the protest and all gave rise to the feeling that the police may have planned to kill John Soto. If they did not, then John was another victim of the gun mentality of the police. The neighborhood was tense and suspicious, and the next day, a two-year-old girl, Rosina Marbley, was shot by police who were shooting at snipers in the Cabrini-Green Projects. Summer had ended, but the tensions between police and the community continued, even heightened.

John's 21-year-old brother, Michael, was an Army sergeant and a war hero. He'd been witness to the oppression of the Vietnamese also. Home on leave, he too was involved in the fight for the stoplight. In fact, he was one of those arrested in the stoplight protests. The death of his brother, yet another police killing in the neighborhood of Mile Square, spawned the Robinson House Committee to End the Murder of Black People, with Michael Soto as a member. They called for an investigation into brother John's death. Michael asked for an extension on his leave to arrange for his brother's funeral.[63]

On Friday, October 10, 1969, there was, supposedly, a robbery near the Projects, and the suspects were chased into the buildings. That's the police version. Patrolman Robert Rahn chased Michael Soto to a landing of the Project building and shot him dead. Witnesses say he was standing on the landing talking to police when the officer killed him. This officer had killed another teenager a week before. Witnesses say Michael was unarmed; the officer says he killed in self-defense. Both Soto brothers, the most easily identifiable participants in a civil rights protest (because they did not look like the others), were now dead. This would seem to indicate a police hit squad at work.

As Michael Soto lay dying, police converged on the scene, while at the same time, the word of his murder spread throughout the Projects.

Older folks, who seemed to be the most conservative people on earth to young black radicals, didn't respond to talk of revolution, but, in the tradition of Mississippi farmers (or sharecroppers), pushed too far by the Klan, the residents of Henry Horner responded to this death. When they heard of Michael Soto's death, they went for their guns. The women stepped aside and let the "brothers" go ahead. The Panthers had shown them that the police were not supermen; now they used the knowledge. For two hours, bullets rained on police and squad cars. The police retaliated with indiscriminate fire into the Projects. When the shooting subsided, nine police were injured, and the police had accidentally killed an 11-year-old girl.[64]

In the weeks that followed, eyewitnesses to the Soto brothers' deaths were harassed out of the neighborhood.[65] Again, spontaneous organizations formed to fight police oppression. The Panthers called for a decentralized, community-controlled police force.

The investigations into the killings were hampered, according to the State's Attorney's (Ed Hanrahan's) office, by the distrust of black people for the State and the District Attorney. Somehow, said the State's Attorney's people and the F.B.I., the neighborhood residents felt the State's Attorney and the Police Department were one and the same. Well, the facts substantiate residents' beliefs. Of some 79 cases of police killings of civilians in 1969-70 (including the Soto brothers, either eye-witness accounts of police killing citizens, nor evidence that contradicted the police, or contradictions between police, brought one single policeman to court.[66] Yet the Cook County State's Attorney had reviewed *every single* case. Early the next year, State's Attorney Hanrahan dropped the case, blaming the community's lack of trust in his office. At the same time, he was, in fact, acting with the police to cover up a murderous shoot-out by Chicago police assigned to his office.

**Jake Winters, November 13, 1969.** The killing of the Soto brothers in October re-emphasized, for the members of the Black Panther Party, what they could expect at the hands of the police if they were ever caught at night. It underlined the tension and anger and came at a traumatic time for 19-year-old Jake Winters. The Panther Party had become Jake's life. He believed in it totally, saw its effects on ghetto youth, and immersed himself in it. Around the end of the first week of November, however, Jake and his cadre's leader, Bobby Rush, had a serious disagreement. By temperament, Jake was fiery, active, and direct, whereas Rush was low-key, moderate. Rush wanted Jake expelled after this altercation over Party policies, and he had his way. It was a bitter pill for Jake to swallow. Now, one week later, when he should have been getting his head together for the college scholarship he'd received for Xavier University, he was instead walking around the South Side neighborhood of his boyhood, distraught and angry.

Jake was hanging with Lance "Santa Claus" Bell, a Party member, and they had an argument with a man who was a jail guard at the "County." The man had taken a pistol from them, and they were demanding it back. They hung around his house on 58th and Calumet, waiting for him that night. His wife got nervous and called the police, while Jake went into the abandoned Washington Park Hotel on the southeast corner of 58th, which he and some friends used for a hangout. When the police arrived, they came down 58th Street from the east, surrounding the building from the side Jake could not see. Had they come from the west or down Calumet, he would have seen them early and perhaps fled. Now the building was surrounded and he was trapped. Of course, Jake was aware of what had happened to the Soto Brothers and what had apparently happened to Larry Roberson in jail. And in his hideout, Jake kept at least two guns, plenty of ammunition. And Jake knew guns well. The situation was loaded, weighted down by the history of police in the ghetto that summer.

Once Jake found himself trapped, his actions indicated the intensity of his rage. He had witnessed, almost intimately, the deaths of over a dozen black people at the hands of the Chicago police that summer. The city, the courts, the D.A. had done nothing about them. Now Jake had a chance. As the first police officer approached the abandoned building, Jake fired his carbine, and the officer was killed. Then, as more and more police arrived, Jake ran from room to room, firing bursts of automatic fire and single shots. He virtually demolished five police cars and wounded nine police. They fired back at what appeared to be three or four people. One war veteran said it was hotter than any fight he'd seen in Vietnam. Jake was wounded and bleeding badly about twenty minutes after the fight began when he escaped from the gangway exit north of the old building into the cold, snow-flurried night, heading north to the alley and then down toward 59th. His wound left a clear trail, picked up by pursuing police. It led into a dark backyard with a tunnel under the building to the street, King Drive. Jake went through, climbed the porch steps on the left side of the tunnel, and waited, shotgun in his hand, loaded and ready. No mercy plea, no running away; he'd end it all here tonight. The first police officer came through the gangway tunnel, and Jake blasted away. And as the officer begged for his life, Jake dropped into the gangway and blasted away a second time. The next policeman through the gangway killed Jake and then, in an expression of fury, pumped round after round into Jake's lifeless body.

It was stunning. One 19-year-old, never trained by the military, on his own grounds, had handled scores of police for twenty minutes and led one into a deadly trap. Here was something unprecedented in Chicago. That "boy" hadn't acted like a "nigger;" he'd acted more like an old-time rebel, maybe one of Quantrill's boys, happy to die while putting lead into his enemy. "What the hell was changing these niggers?" the Dixicrats may have asked. In Chicago, it was the Panther Party. It gave them intense pride.

**Killing the last leader.** The night after the Jake Winters shootout, F.B.I. agent Roy Mitchell of the Chicago office and his informant in the Panther Party, William O'Neal, talked about the shootout. Mitchell had some gruesome photos on hand, which reportedly showed what O'Neal's "friends" in the Party had done to the two slain policemen. Mitchell evidently was meeting with some resistance from O'Neal and pressuring him for more intimate information on Fred Hampton. One gets the impression that O'Neal was busy both lying to the F.B.I. and deceiving the Panthers, as a regular course of action, hoping not to get caught in this game by his "friends" in the Party, while not giving the F.B.I. anything useful. Mitchell was twisting the screws down now, however, and O'Neal was caught. On November 19th, he returned to the F.B.I. with a detailed map of the apartment Fred Hampton rented under the name of Fred Johnson at 2337 W. Monroe. The map included an arrow that showed where Chairman Fred slept. O'Neal insisted that Mitchell do nothing until he (O'Neal) was notified, but he must have realized how weak that appeal was.

Fred's apartment on Monroe, one block south of Panther headquarters, was also a sleeping place for several of the remaining central staff when they were not in jail or on the move. Together, Mitchell and O'Neal filled out the map showing furniture, doors, and rooms.[67] Mitchell then passed the map on to Gang Intelligence, Chicago Police, and a list of legally purchased weapons in the apartment and urged a raid. At least, that's his story. Gang Intelligence, on the other hand, says two of the weapons he mentioned were sawed-off shotguns. And so they scheduled a raid for November 24th or 25th. Somewhere, there was a leak in the plans. Was it O'Neal or a member of the police? This we don't know and may never know, but however it happened, the Panther Party learned they were to be raided, removed all their weapons and left two

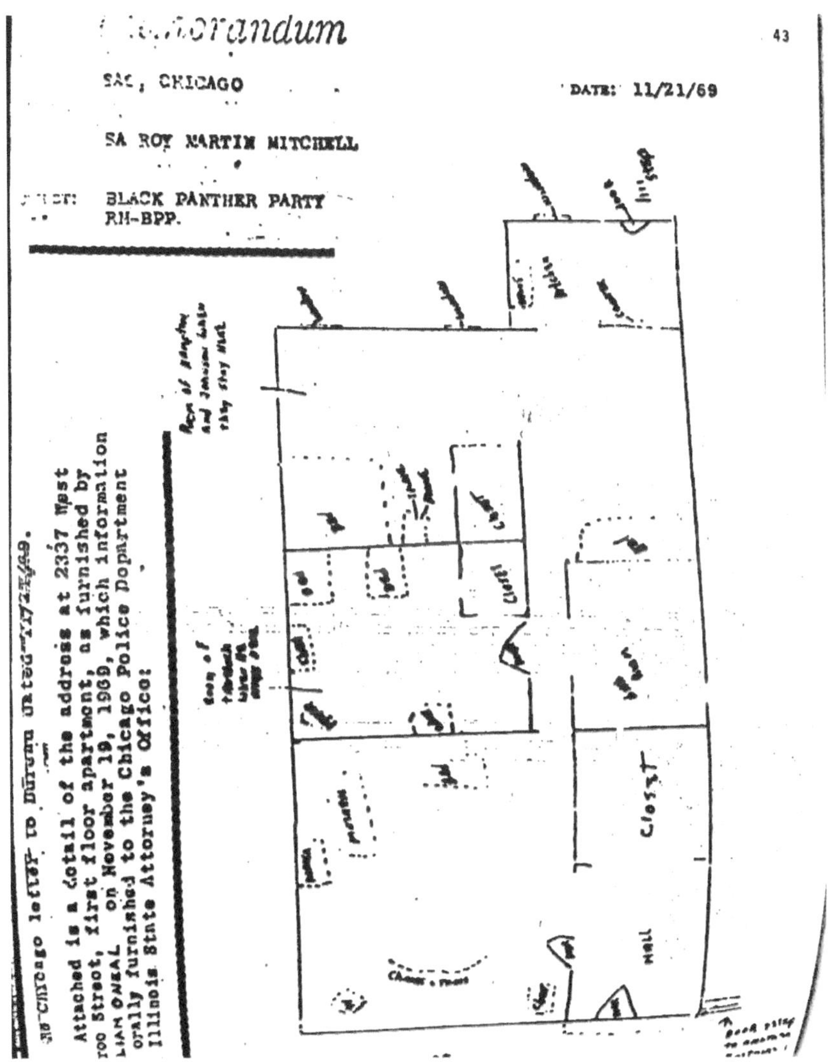
Memorandum
43
SAC, CHICAGO
DATE: 11/21/69
SA ROY MARTIN MITCHELL
BLACK PANTHER PARTY
RM-BPP.
RE: Chicago letter to Bureau dated 11/21/69.

Attached is a detail of the address at 2337 West
roo Street, first floor apartment, as furnished by
LIAM ONEAL on November 19, 1969, which information
orally furnished to the Chicago Police Department
Illinois State Attorney's Office:
Closet
Closet
Mall

women and two movie cameras to greet the raiders. That they were aware
of the raid also leaked back to the police—probably through O'Neal.

The raid was canceled and the Party evidently found out about that,
and so the weapons were moved back in.

The Party was in bad shape, and Fred was taxed to his limit, trying
to keep up with the dwindling Party and increasing work. There was
never a more isolated moment for the Party than that winter of '69 prior
to December 4th. The central staff was virtually nonexistent; loss in
members, particularly in leaders, weakened its dependability and hurt
discipline. And Fred had only a short time to work before he'd be back
in jail, for his appeal on the ice cream truck robbery in Maywood, what
must have seemed like ages ago, was denied.

The F.B.I. and the police were aware of the schedule that Fred and the
remaining Party members kept at the apartment. Monday, Wednesday,
and Friday evening, they went a few blocks away for political education
classes at the People's Church on Ashland. If they had wanted to simply
seize weapons, that was the ideal time for a raid. But that clearly was not
what they wanted, and everyone was well aware of it. Field Lieutenant
Jewell Cook told Fred when he returned to Chicago in late November
that it was absolutely necessary that Fred move—revenge (for the Jake
Winters shootout) was in the wind. They began to work on tighter
security, putting up a floodlight above the back steps and building an
escape hatch in the closet by Fred's bed. The escape hatch was to lead
next door, but as of December 4th, it led outside. The floodlight was up,
but they couldn't get it working. Circumstances were turning against the
Party's leader living through the winter.

F.B.I. agent Roy Mitchell now called the Cook County State's
Attorney Edward Hanrahan and suggested a raid on the Party's leader.
Hanrahan, an ambitious man already written up in the media as a man
warring on the "gangs," took to the idea. He had assigned to him a small
contingent of Chicago police.

Hanrahan and assistant Jalovec began to implement the raid. They
collected volunteers and sent one of them, "Gloves" Davis, to look
the apartment over. They got a search warrant, which included those
nonexistent sawed-off shotguns—though another spy besides O'Neal, one
Maria Fisher, confirmed that all weapons at the apartment were legal.[68]
(Maria, a Haitian, hung around the Panthers, expressing a desire to them
that they assassinate "Papa Doc" of Haiti.)

They planned the raid for December 4th at 5:00 a.m., when they figured it would be occupied and the occupants asleep. They would use fourteen armed men in plainclothes, armed with 27 weapons, including a machine gun, several shotguns, and an automatic carbine—no tear gas, no loudspeakers. The raiders themselves included a cop with a reputation for violent misbehavior and two who were friends of the cops killed by Jake Winters. Clearly, they planned for this to be a violent raid, and then there was the map of the apartment showing where Fred Hampton slept. Seemingly, an assassination was laid out—if only some raider would pick up on it.

That evening, the arrested Minister of Information was put in the "hole" at Cook County Jail. Fred's bodyguard, Cleve, was in an Indiana jail with a half-million dollar bond for a petty theft charge; the local militant youth group, known as the Black Liberation Army, who were believed to be the boys who had made it hot for the killers of the Soto brothers, were on a winter retreat in Michigan, sponsored by either the YMCA or a government agency. The National Guard was put on alert, Illinois Bell provided a van for the police to approach the apartment camouflaged, and at 3:00 a.m., they moved.

Fred, Deborah Johnson, eight months pregnant with his child, and ten other Party members had returned to the apartment about midnight. Mark Clark, one of them, was the leader of the Peoria branch of the Illinois Black Panther Party and, like Fred, was a promising leader. Mark came from a well-known Peoria family. His father was a prominent minister in Peoria; one of his sisters, Patricia, was homecoming queen at Illinois State University. Mark had taken his small cadre of Panthers and organized a free breakfast for children program on Peoria's impoverished South Side (called "the valley"). He'd also gone up "on the hill" to Bradley University to sell Panther papers and collect donations. He'd been arrested for that. Peoria was a conservative town, a town beginning to have racial problems, full of refugees from the warfare in Cairo, Illinois, where Klan violence made for dangerous racial antagonisms. Still, Peoria wasn't any more ready for revolution than Chicago. That Peoria had a Panther Party at all was due to Mark Clark, an 18-year-old with leadership qualities.

After a late dinner, Fred and Deborah retired to the rear bedroom as usual. Bobby Rush, William O'Neal, and two other Party members left for their homes. The rest divided between the other bedroom and the living room in the front. Fred called his mother and went to sleep in the middle of the conversation. Later, O'Neal was said to have bragged how he'd drugged Fred by slipping a drug in his Kool-Aid.

About 4:30 a.m., police pulled up to the apartment at 2337 W. Monroe. Eight went to the front door of the first-floor apartment, and six went to the back. The block was sealed off by other police as the fourteen officers climbed the stairs. The woman who lived upstairs from Fred heard a knock at the front door below her. She said she heard someone say, "Open up, police." There was a pause—then all hell broke loose. A shot exploded at the front door, followed by machine gunfire and bursts from other guns. As the shooting began in the front, it was followed by shooting in the rear of the apartment. For a full ten minutes, a barrage of fire was heard—screams and more fire.

What happened can, for the most part, be pieced together from the physical evidence left. Clearly, the police burst into the door and found an extra door, one not on their map. Here, a shotgun went off, and another. One was Mark Clark's. Whether he fired first or his gun went off as he was killed, the undisputed fact is he was standing behind that extra door as a guard; he was shot through the heart and killed, and no other Panther Party member fired a single shot. In the front room, Brenda Harris was evidently reaching for a weapon when she was shot twice and disabled, then the wall behind her was stitched with bullets from a machine gun. Brenda, called "China Doll" by her friends because of her doll-like face, shot at the police according to them, yet her gun was never fired, nor were any bullet holes coming at them from that direction; lost in a sky hook, the police say.

As the first shots rang out from the front, six police burst in the back door. They say they were fired on, but the physical evidence proves no shots were fired at them. At the same time, the layout of the apartment tends to show that Officer Davis, firing from a prone position in the front living room, could appear to be shooting at them. Strangely, however, they never fired back in his direction. In fact, all the firing heads in the same direction, toward Fred Hampton's bedroom.

As the firing died down, the police could see four people in Fred's bedroom. Two, Louis Truelock and Harold Bell, had been trying to wake Fred ever since the first knock on the door. They were grabbed out and made to lie on the floor and handcuffed. Deborah came out with her hands up. The police had now captured the apartment; Mark Clark was dead, Brenda Harris was wounded. And, evidence supports the conclusion that Fred had not been seriously wounded because Deborah, who was sleeping next to Fred in her nightgown, was later that day photographed in that gown, a photo that shows a clean, bloodless gown, in contrast to the mattress on which Fred died, which was soaked with blood that flowed even onto the floor. The shooting evidently resumed into the other middle bedroom, wounding Party Minister of Health Ronald Satchel six times and an unlucky visiting friend twice. Once this firing stopped, a firing that may have wounded or killed Fred, the Party members say, they heard a policeman in Fred's room say, "He's alive; he'll barely make it." Then, two more shots and the voice added, "He's good and dead now." Fred Hampton, 21, was dead. The cause of death was two small caliber bullets in the head, fired from above. The raiders left, taking the Panthers in cuffs, their weapons, but leaving the building wide open. The Panthers, still free, returned and opened the apartment to the public for viewing.

State's Attorney Hanrahan, under criticism almost immediately for the violent methods used, had his police act out their version of the raid. Their version had the police under heavy fire, begging the Panthers to surrender, to which the only reply from the Panthers was, "Shoot it out!" From where the Panthers supposedly shot, there are no shells; the direction in which they supposedly shot left no bullet holes in the walls or the doors; no police were hit, yet *CBS* runs this story on the evening news. The surviving Party members are charged with attempted murder, and everyone tries to pretend that nothing has happened (business as usual in the ghetto).

But Fred had many allies, had support from a wide base, and was admired by respected professionals, people who knew how dangerous a stand he had taken. Immediately, a group of lawyers was working for the Party, and what they were able to prove smelled—like murder. Ninety-nine bullets were fired on that raid, and 98 were traced to a policeman's gun.

The so-called leaders of the ghetto (how can a ghetto have its own leadership?), although a far cry from Panther supporters, realized a dangerous precedent had been set. After all, the police hadn't secretly gotten rid of an enemy; they'd blatantly killed him, asleep in his bed. If they could do that to a man for talking radical, they can get rid of radical talk altogether, and then moderate talk becomes radical. So they moved to support the Panther Party. Besides, they did admire Fred, and deep down must have known much of what he said was nothing but truth; suicidal, they may have thought, but true. And the issues were still very much alive, like poverty, despair, crime. We've got the right to sit on the front of the bus in Alabama, but here in the North, we are still the last hired, first fired, segregated, and ghettoized. The Black Panther Party deals with these issues and offers a radical alternative. And of course,  that is also why all they will get from most people is financial support; physical support is dangerous.

However, the attitude of disrespect for black people that the system has shown by the killing of Fred brought explosive, emotional support for the Party from young people all over the city—largely blacks and Latinos, but whites also. Youth is disgusted with the city and expressed it on the first anniversary of Fred's death, December 4, 1970. Deputy Minister of Defense Bobby Rush called for a high school boycott and showed the muscle his Party had gathered. The boycott went off as planned. At Crane High, near Panther headquarters, the entire student body came to school just so they could walk out and, on cue, 1,300 marched out. Teachers, police were helpless to stop it. The same happens at Harlan High, Hyde Park, Englewood, Calumet, and South Shore. All of those who bothered to come walked out of Kenwood, Dunbar, Phillips, Marshall, Bowen, Harrison, Fenger, and Austin. Students and police clashed at Calumet, and at Chicago Vocational School, CVS, a riot between 1,000 students and police went up and down 87th Street. But the students didn't just take a holiday. Five thousand attended two rallies honoring Fred.

Today, there are no youth groups in radical politics or serving the people free breakfast, free medical services, or free transportation to visit prisons as there were in those Panther years. The youth movement was killed by a thorough job of surveillance, disruption, and media propaganda, which is detailed in Part II.

> Don't worry about the Black Panther Party. As long as you
> keep the beat, we'll keep on going. If you think that we can
> be wiped out because they murdered Bobby Hutton and
> Alprentice Bunchy Carter and John Huggins, you're wrong.
> If you think that because Huey was jailed the Party's gonna
> stop, you see you're wrong. If you think because Chairman
> Bobby was jailed the Party's gonna stop, you see you're wrong
> ... because we said it before we left and we said it today. That
> you can jail a revolutionary but you can't jail the revolution.

You can lock up a freedom fighter like Huey P. Newton, but you can't lock up freedom fighting. You might hire some pork chops like Mamlama to murder Alprentice Bunchy Carter, a liberator, but you can't murder liberation, because if you do, you come up with answers that don't answer, explanations that don't explain, conclusions that don't conclude.

# NOTES ON THE ILLINOIS BLACK PANTHER PAST, AS OF 2026

It is late November 1969.  Five or six members of the Illinois Panther Party are sitting on the 2nd floor of Panther Headquarters, and Ronald "Doc" Satchel voices the opinion that William O'Neal is a "pig," an informant. Someone nods their head, and another says, "Damned right." What is it about O'Neal?  He's a lot negative, he says so-and-so is jive, she's too bourgey, that niggah's full of shit, etc.  He's quick to label people who come around the Party as spies.  He comes up with ideas like "Let's raid the white neighborhood, with the next riot." Negativity is not unusual in a poor black community. It can get in your blood at an early age.  Maybe it's your uncle saying, "You ain't nothing and you ain't gonna amount to nothing." My uncle never said that. Luck of the draw, I guess. But this negative was unusual around the Panthers in 1969. It was there, but that wasn't the overall vibe. I was there, let me tell you.

Fred said, "What we doing? We feeding 4,000 children a day and moving on to providing free health care for your community.  Serve the people!" Fred said, "What we doing?  We serving the people!"

Then Chairman Fred was killed, asleep in his bed. Dead from a police raid that shows, by the pattern of the bullets fired, that the police knew where Fred slept in that apartment.  And, COINTELPRO did not stop there.  O'Neal was still there. No one knew who had provided information to the police. Anyone could be next.

O'Neal targeted Gerald Dunigan, got his wife hooked on drugs, and then O.D.'d her. "I know who did it," he told Dunigan. He pointed out an innocent couple that lived in Sandburg Village. Gerald Dunigan followed them, broke into their apartment, shot the man and beat his wife senseless. He says he flipped out and did not remember the entire incident. Gerald Dunigan went to jail to serve 800 years for attempted murder.

Imagine yourself a Chicago Panther, in the midst of January 1970. You are still harassed, and now, you're glancing at your comrades. Suspicion was the poison of the morale of the organization.

The Illinois Black Panther Party did not end in December of 1969. However, the nature and the aura of the Party changed. The people of your community, that Miles Square community, pulled back. It was too much to deal with.

The Illinois Black Panther Party moved from the West Side of Chicago to Bronzeville on the South Side. The Party moved away from a people who were largely unrepresented in traditional city politics, where independent organizations in politics and in social services were run by people independent of the Cook County Democratic Party. West Siders had been organizing through local people, through home-grown organizations like the Deacons for Defense and Justice, Search for Truth, the West Side Organization, the Midwest Community Council. The Catholic Church, in its most radical form, i.e., clergy (nuns and priests), young idealist socialist clergy, I mean. And, women of the Presbyterian church had a presence on the West Side. As did local churches born in the South. Protestant black ministers in 1960 were preaching from independent pulpits, be they Baptist, Church of God in Christ, Church of God, or jackleg preachers set up in abandoned shops. Urbanization had taken root, but not the attempts at political control of those institutions. For that decade of the 1960s, the black West Side was the natural home of revolutionaries. "Revolution is the solution" made sense in that decade and in that place, culminating in the events of October through December of 1969, and on into the first two years of the 1970s.

Setting up Deputy Chairman Fred Hampton for assassination was the culmination of the federal government's program to stamp out the threat of revolutionary change. But that assassination was equally amenable to the Democratic Party for the more limited goal of stifling independent thinking politics, thinking outside the two-party system–which in Chicago was actually a one-party system. Imagine the politically elected State's Attorney Edward Hanrahan being presented with the idea of killing the leader of a black revolutionary movement whose organization was successfully serving an unrepresented community in Chicago. Would Edward Hanrahan take charge of that assassination on his own, or would he take it to his boss? We don't know, but we can guess.

Serving over 4,000 hungry children breakfast every day, then offering free health care. All this without a cent of government funding. "What are we doing?" Fred said. "We are serving the people." Maybe the wind starts to whisper, we can do for ourselves. Now that attitude had to be stamped out, and O'Neal could kill it, wrapped in Black ego. Two spirits like that cannot co-exist. The government fed money. Omawale, Charles Robertson, Jake Winters, dead, a pregnant woman beaten in Altgeld Gardens, tipped the scale, at least for now.

Chicago's South Side, from Bronzeville to Altgeld Gardens, had undergone an urbanization and acculturation over the decades. The Cook County Democratic Party showed little tolerance for independent political thought on either side of town, but they had suppressed it thoroughly on the South Side, so that challenges to its hegemony were, by the 1960s, handled with a gloved fist. The days of white communists coming into Bronzeville in 1930, and being beaten by Chicago Police just for being there, were fading memories and not talked about by 1960. Our parents remembered that being a communist sympathizer could get you in trouble, so they didn't talk about it. The days of two-gun Pete, the black police officer who killed twelve young black men in his eleven years on the force in the 1940s, were also gone. But "Gloves" Davis still roamed the West Side. The Black communists were old and sidelined. The Klan and the Outfit were still in the CPD, but not as obvious on the South Side. Opposition to Dr. King in 1966 came from the South Side, not the West Side. The conservative approach to change, i.e., gradual change, like a glacier, had a field for growth in the relative success of the middle-class black community. What the far South Side politicians, including nationalists, wanted was protection for newly achieved gains. They wanted affirmative action, they wanted DEI, and government money.

So, the revolutionary Black Panther Party on Indiana Avenue was out of its element in Bronzeville, where politically active Black Nationalism had taken root as the radical end of political change. When you think Black Nationalism, think of China under Chiang Kai-shek, an independent Chinese-run capitalism. It made sense for middle-class objectives. Any Southsider professional reading the Panthers' Ten-Point Program would not be appreciative.

The community of Miles Square, on the West Side in 1968, would rally around Black Panthers nailing up a stop sign in front of Henry

Horner Homes to get protection for the toddlers and youngsters crossing the street. Southsiders would go to their alderman. Either way is to do what works best in your neighborhood. All-black West Side wards had all-white precinct captains.

So, Bobby Rush, one of the Illinois Chapter's founders and leader, was still at the helm and by 1971, he had a new road to map. He would have to engage traditional South Side politics and would, eventually.

Every move the Black Panther Party made in Bronzeville from 1971 through 1974,  to serve the community, was done under the observation of the local people, paid off by a precinct captain or alderman. Then, money was put out to disrupt service programs. The bus to take parents to see their jailed relatives was disabled where it was parked more than once. Panther headquarters was raided for a supposed bomb, which was in fact a large bologna sausage donated for the free breakfast program. Local people or a person saw the shape and phoned it in.

How do you form relationships with the local people when the locals are aware that the government is watching you and that law enforcement will harass and arrest anyone? That wasn't West Side politics. That was Cold War politics of the federal government.

How effective could you be in what was left of the organization? People left the Panther Party, as they realized they could be more effective elsewhere.

At the same time, the Oakland headquarters wanted Chicago's talent and resources and took them. Billy Brooks, the Deputy Minister of Education, was sent to Oakland for a year.

Still, the end of the Black Panther Party in Chicago was not a foregone conclusion. A core of the original Party hung on to serve free breakfasts and provide visits to Illinois prisons. There was, in the last years, a defense committee for a group of young men known as the De Mau Mau. Had they been the group that murdered people, or were they being railroaded? It seems to have been a mixed bag; some were, and perhaps some were not.  The Panthers who remained were courageously still serving the people, and the Party still had talented, dedicated people, but the Party was no longer a vibrant place to serve.

So, to understand the beauty and the functionality of the Illinois Black Panther Party at its height is to imagine the courage of those first two years of its existence. It was then, in the late 1960s, when some of the bravest of that generation of youthful idealists took on the task of daring to confront a system built for the greed of those who have too much already and are willing to enforce their avaricious ways with violence and divide and conquer. These men and women, young then, risked their lives for a revolution based on sharing the power; power to all people as equals, with a dream to live and share abundantly in a new society, a revolutionary society, a society where the people mattered, all lives mattered, whose theme was "All Power to the People."

That dream sleeps at the curb, brushing up the leaves while the wind of world domination drives on.

# ENDNOTES


1       Mrs. Harris, an official at Chicago Board of Education, Administrative Department, 1978.

2       *The New York Times*, October 23, 1963, p. 1.

3       Ibid., February 6, 1964, p. 20.

4       Ibid., February 26, 1964, p. 24.

5       Ibid., March 3, 1964, p. 23.

6       Ibid., July 1, 1965, p. 27.

7       Interview with civil rights marcher activist David Finke, Fall, 1980.

8       Ibid.

9       George Breitman, editor, *Malcolm X Speaks* (Grove Press, 1965), pp. 163-165. For more on Malcolm's stand on violence and non-violence, see pp. 144-46 and Malcolm X Speaking, Ethnic Records, April 1965.

10      "Brother Malcolm: His Theme Now Is Violence," U.S. News and World Report, Volume 56, March 23, 1964, p. 19.

11      Letter written by Helen Mascio, June 6, 1966. Also see Chicago American, Sunday, June 12, 1966, p. 4, section 1.

12      Interview with Phil Cohran, Summer, 1981.

13      Interview with former President, Lutheran Human Relations Association of Maywood, February 23, 1978.

14      Isaac Balbus, *The Dialectic of Legal Repression* (Russell Sage Foundation, 1973) pp. 175- 188.

15      Frederick Thrasher, *The Gang, A Study of 1,313 Gangs in Chicago* (University of Chicago Press, 1963 reprint), pp. 15-16.

16      Ibid., p. 139.

17      Ibid., p. 139.

18      *Newsweek*, June 5, 1967.

19      *Time Magazine*, July 5, 1968.

20      J. David Greenstone and Paul Peterson, *Race and Authority in Urban Politics* (Russell Sage Foundation, 1973), p. 22

21      Peter Knauss, *Chicago: A One-Party State*, p. 116.

22      John Fish, *Black Power/White Control* (Princeton U. Press, 1973).

23      U.S. Senate, 2nd Session, Report No. 94-755, *Final Report of the Select Committee to Study Government Operations with Respect to Intelligence Activities, Supplemental Detailed Staff Reports, Book III*, p. 197; [Hereafter referred to as *Book III, Church Report.*]

24      Ibid., p. 197.

25      *Chicago Defender,* May 29, 1969.

26      Philip Foner, *The Black Panthers Speak* (Lippincott, 1970), p. 139.

27      Ibid., p. 140.

28      Interview with police officer from Afro-American Police League.

29      Jerome Skolnick, Director, *The Politics of Protest* (Clarion Books, 1969), p. 255.

30      *Chicago Sun-Times*, December 28, 1967, p. 4.

31      Op. cit., Skolnick, pp. 260, 263.

32      *Chicago Sun-Times*, December 29, 1967, p. 1.

33      *The Chicago Defender*, May 6, 1969.

34      Ibid., May 1, 1969 and May 8, 1969.

35      Ibid., May 13, 1969.

36      Ralph Knoohuizen, et al., *The Police and Their Fatal Use of Force in Chicago* (Knoohuizen, 1972), p. 32.

37      Ibid., Index Wayne Black file.

38      Ibid., Index 34, Maple Shorten file.

39      Interview with Howard Saffold of the AAPL

40      *Chicago Defender*, October 7, 1969.

41      Howard Saffold interview.

42      Michael Arden, *An American Verdict*. (New York: Doubleday, 1973).

43      *The Black Panther Community News*, August 23, 1969, p. 25.

44      The Brief for Plaintiff Appellants Anderson, Bell, Clark, Satchel, Truelock, No. 77-1698. Appeals from the U.S. District Court for the Northern District of Illinois, Eastern Division, p. 10. [Hereafter this source is referred to as The Appeal Brief.]

45      Ibid., p. 10.

46      Interviews with Minister of Defense Black Panther Party, and with another Party member.

47      Milton Rakove, *Don't Make No Waves, Don't Back No Losers* (University of Indiana Press, 1975).

48      Interview with Minister of Education, Black Panther Party.

49      *The Black Panther*, August 16, 1969, p. 28.

50      Interview with Panther Party member.

51      Interview with former Party members present at the raid.

52      *You've Got to Make a Commitment,* an uncopyrighted collection of Fred Hampton's speeches, probably in 1970. Printed.

53      *Chicago Sun-Times,* June 5, 1969, p. 40.

54      Ibid., October 16, 1972.

55      Ibid., June 11, 1969,p.6.

56      Ibid., May 16, 1970.

57      Op cit., Knoohuizen, index.

58      Op cit., Isaac Balbus, p. 167.

59      *Chicago Daily News*, November 13, 1969.

60      George Breitman, editor, *Malcolm X Speaks*, pp. 165-66.

61      Philip Foner, *The Black Panthers Speak*, p. 140.

62      *Chicago Defender,* November 22-28, 1969, and *Chicago Sun-Times*, March 2, 1970.

63      *Chicago Sun-Times*, March 2, 1970, p. 28.

64      *Chicago Daily Defender*, October 14, 1969.

65      Ibid., November 22-28,1969.

66      The Appeal Brief, p. 36-A.

67      Ibid., p. 35.

68      Ibid., p. 140.

# BIBLIOGRAPHY

## BOOKS


Alinsky, Saul. *Radicals in Urban Politics: The Alinsky Approach*, University of Chicago Press, 1974.

Arden, Michael. *An American Verdict*, Doubleday, 1973.

Balbus, Isaac. *The Dialectic of Legal Repression, Black Rebels before the American Criminal Courts*, Russell Sage Foundation, 1973.

Baruch, Ruth-Marian and Jones, Pickle, *The Vanguard, A Photo-Graphic Essay on the Black Panthers*, Beacon Press, 1970.

Breitman, George, editor. *Malcolm X Speaks: Selected Speeches and Statements*, Grove Press, 1966.

Brown, H. Rap. *Die Nigger, Die*. Dial Press, 1970.

Chicago Commission on Race Relations, editor. *The Negro in Chicago: A Study of Race Relations and a Race Riot*, Arno Press, 1968 (reprint of 1922).

Cleaver, Elderidge. *Soul on Ice*, Dell, 1968.

Conot, Robert. *Rivers of Blood, Years of Darkness*, William Morrow, 1968.

Davis, Angela and Aptheker, Bettina, editors. *If They Come in the Morning*, New American Library, 1971.

Demaris, Ovid. *Captive City*, Lyle Stuart, Inc., 1969.

Duncan, Otis and Duncan, Beverly. *The Negro Population in Chicago*, University of Chicago Press, 1957.

Editors of Ebony. *Ebony Pictorial History of Black America*, Johnson Publishing Company, 1971 (three volumes).

Fish, John H., *Black Power I White Control: The Stuggle of TWO in Chicago*, Princeton University Press, 1973.

Foner, Philip S. *The Black Panthers Speak*, Lippincott, 1970.

Freed, Leonard. *Black in White America*, Grossman Publishers, 1967.

International Library of Negro Life. *1968: The Year of Awakening, The Association for the Study of Negro Life and History*, 1969.

Kardiner, A. and Ovesey, Lionel. *The Mark of Oppression: Explorations in the Personality of the American Negro*, 1951.

Keiser, R.L *Vice Lords: Warriors of the Streets*, Holt, Rinehart & Winston, 1969.

Knauss, Peter. *Chicago: A One-Party State*, University of Illinois Press, 1972.

Knatznelson, Ira. *Black Men, White Cities, Race. Politics and Migration in the U.S. 1900-30 and Britain 1948-68*, Columbia, 1973.

* Knoohuizen, Ralph, et. al., *The Police and Their Fatal Use of Force in Chicago*, Knoohuizen, 1972.

Lader, Lawrence. *Power on the Left, American Radical Movements Since 1946*, Norton, 1979.

Lait, Jack and Mortimer, Lee, *Chicago Confidential*, Avon Publishers, 1950.

Malcolm X, assisted by Alex Haley. *The Autobiography of Malcolm X*, Grove, 1964.

Mao, Tse-Tung, *Quotations from Chairman Mau Tse-Tung*, Foreign Languages Press, Peking, 1967.

Marine, Gene. *The Black Panthers*, New American Library, 1969.

Mayer, Harold and Wade, Richard. *Chicago: Growth of a Metropolis*, University of Chicago Press, 1969.

Millea, Thomas. *Ghetto Fever*, Glencoe Press, 1968.

Novak, Michael. *Rise of the Unmeltable Ethnics*, Macmillan, 1972.

Peterson, Paul. *School Politics Chicago Style*, University of Chicago Press, 1976.

Priam Books. *The Trial of Bobby Seale*. Priam Books, 1970.

Quarles, Benjamin. *The Negro in the Making of America*, Collier, 1964.

Rakove, Milton. *Don't Make No Waves, Don't Back No Losers*, Indiana University Press, 1975.

Robinson, Stanley. *The Badge They Are Trying to Bury*, Simon Belt Publishers, 1975.

Rustin, Bayard. *Strategies for Freedom*, Columbia University Press, 1976.

Seale, Bobby. *Seize the Time*, The Story of the Black Panther Party and Huey Newton, Random House, 1967.

Skolnick, Jerome. *The Politics of Protest*, Simon and Schuster, 1969.
Spear, Allen. Black Chicago, *The Making of a Negro Ghetto 1890-1920*,
University of Chicago, 1969.
Strickland, Arvarh. *A History of the Chicago Urban League*, University of
Illinois Press, 1966.
Terkel, Studs. *Division Street: America*, Pantheon Books, 1967.
Thrasher, Frederick M. *The Gang, A Study of 1,313 Gangs in Chicago*,
University of Chicago Press, 1963 (reprint).
Warner, William. *Colorand Human Nature*, Negro University Press.

## PERIODICALS

*Atlantic Monthly*. "Alone in Cover-Up country," Volume 232, October,
1973.
*Chicago Journalism Review*, "What's It All About Eddie?" December,
1972.
*Ebony Magazine*. "The Gang Phenomenon: Big City Headache," Vol. 22,
No. 10, August, 1967.
________."Black Panthers, Huey P. Newton," Volume 24, August, 1969.
*Life Magazine*. "The Killing of Billy Furr, Caught in the Act of Looting
Beer," July, 1967.
*The Nation*. "Out to Get the Panthers: F.B.I. and the Chicago Police,"
Volume 209, July 28, 1969.
*New Yorker*. "A Reporter at Large, The Panthers and the Police: A Pattern
of Genocide," February 13,1971.
*Newsweek*. "Converting a Gang into Organization Men," Volume 69,
June 5,1967.
________. "Opportunity Please Knock Chorus," Volume 70, Feb. 5,1968.
________. "Panther Hunt," Volume 71, April 22,1968.
________. "Reforming Street Gangs," Volume 72, July 15,1968.
________. "On the Prowl," Volume 72, September 23,1968.
________. "Radicals, Black Panthers in the Vanguard," Volume 74, August
4,1969.
________. "Shoot It Out," Volume 74, December 15,1969.
________. "Too Late for Panthers," Volume 74, December 22,1969.
________."Controversial Verdict," Volume 75, February 2,1970.
________. "Slap on the Wrist," Volume 75, May 25,1970.

________."Philadelphia Guerilla War," Volume 76, September 14,1970.
________. "Double-Agent: Thirteen Harlem Black Panthers on Trial," Volume 76, November 23,1970.
________."Panther Ghost," Volume 78, September 6,1971.
Time Magazine. "Chicago: Gang War," Volume 92, July 5,1968.
________."Police and Panthers at War," Volume 94, December 12,1969.
________. "Panthers' Honky Lawyer," Volume 95, January 12,1970.
________. "The Divided Panthers," Volume 97, February 22,1971.
________. "Verdict for Fast Eddie," Volume 100, November 6,1972.
*U.S. News and World Report.* "Invasion by Armed Black Panthers Sacramento, California," Vol. 62, May 15,1967.
________."We're Going to Shoot the Cops," Volume 63, May 29,1967.

## DOCUMENTS

94th Congress, 2nd Session, Senate Report 94-755, Intelligence Activities and the Rights of Americans, Book II, Senator Frank Church, Chairman.
94th Congress, 2nd Session, Senate Report 94-755, Supplementary Detailed Staff Reports on Intelligence Activities and the Rights of Americans, Book III.
Brief for Plaintiff-Appellants Anderson, Bell, Clark, Satchell, Truelock, No. 77-1698, Appeals from the U.S. District Court for the Northern District of Illinois, Eastern Division, Appeal No. 70-C-1384, J. Sam Perry, Judge.
Tapes from the State of Illinois Senate Legislative Hearings on Police Brutality, Senator R. Newhouse presiding, Summer, 1969.

## RESEARCH PAPERS

Willis, Daniel Joseph. "A Critical Analysis of Mass Political Education and Community Organization as Utilized by the Black Panther Party," University of Massachusetts, 1976, unpublished doctoral dissertation.
Wintersmith, Robert Frazier, "Police and the Black Community," Brandeis University., 1973, unpublished doctoral dissertation.

## NEWSPAPERS

*The Black Panther Community News.* July 5, 1969; July 12, 1969; July 19, 1969; August 23, 1969; November, 1969; February 13,1969; March 12,1977.
*The Chicago American.* June 12,1966.
*The Chicago Daily Defender* and *The Chicago Defender.* November 1, 1967; May 1, 1969; May 6-8, 1969; May 13, 14, 15, 1969; May 20, 1969; May 29, 1969; June 5, 1969; July 1, 1969; July 2, 3, 7, 8, 9, 1969; July 17, 1969; July 23, 1969; October 7, 1969; November 22,28,1969; December 14,1969; December 13,1977.
*The Chicago Daily News.* August 1,1969; July 31, 1969; October 6,1969; October 7, 9, 15, 1969; July 20,25,26,30,1970.
*The Chicago Sun-Times.* December 28, 29, 1967; January 3, 1968; April 1, 1968; April 3, 4, 5, 1969; April 10, 1969; April 15-23, 1969; June 4, 5, 1969; July 16, 1969; August 1, 1969; October 1, 4, 6, 13, 1969; November 13, 1969; December 5, 1969; March 2, 1970; May 4,5,8,1970; May 16, 24,27,28,1970; June 18,19,23,26, 1970; October 18-24,1972; December 1,11,1973; December 24,1974; March 20,1977; January 30,1978; September 2,1978.
*The Chicago Tribune.* April 3, 1955; June 2, 1969; November 24-29. 1974; January 22, 1978; January 30,1978.
*The New York Times.* October 23, 1963; November through December, 1963; February 6, 1964; February 26,1964; July 1,22,1965; January 2,1966; March 17,1966; June 13,1966; August 13, 1966; January 16, 1967; December 29, 1967; January 3, 1968; January 11, 1968; July 6,8,1970; August 16,17,18,19,1970.

## UNCOPYRIGHTED MATERIAL

*You've Got to Make a Commitment*, a booklet collection of Fred Hampton's speeches.

## INTERVIEWS

Interviewee 1 — Founder of National Black Draft Counselors, Chicago

Interviewee 2 — Lawyer for survivors of December 4th Raid

Interviewee 3 — Officer of the Afro-American Patrolmen's League (AAPL)

Interviewee 4 — Officer of the AAPL

Interviewee 5 — Former member of the Black Panther Party, currently a fugitive

Interviewee 6 — Former Minister of Defense of the Illinois Chapter, Black Panther Party

Interviewee 7 — Former Minister of Education, Illinois Black Panther Party

Interviewee 8 — Former student president, Malcolm X City College (1968)

Interviewee 9 — Survivor of the December 4th Raid

Interviewee 10 — Minister of Labor, Illinois Black Panther Party

Interviewee 11— Friend of Fred Hampton and former president of the Lutheran Human Relations Association, Maywood

Interviewee 12 — Lawyer, member of Cook County Bar Association

Interviewee 13 — Former member, Illinois Black Panther Party

Interviewee 14 — Former member, Illinois Black Panther Party

Interviewee 15 — Former head of Chicago C.O.R.E.

Interviewee 16 — Police officer, founder of AAPL

ALSO BY JON F. RICE

*Life in the Shadows of American History*

*Tales of the Martin Clan*

*Black Revolutionaries on Chicago's West Side: A History of the
Illinois Black Panther Party*

# ABOUT THE AUTHOR

Historian Jon F. Rice is a retired educator, first-person historical interpreter, and artist. The middle child of Chicago parents, Rice has spent much of his life studying and interpreting Chicago's history and its communities. His extensive research and first-hand documentation on the Illinois Chapter of the Black Panther Party have been a vital resource for historians, students, and books and films.

Over the course of his career, he taught in Chicago Public Schools, San Diego Unified School District, and the Illinois Department of Corrections, Juvenile Division. He also served as an adjunct professor of history at Roosevelt University, Aurora College, and the University of Massachusetts Boston. Rice earned a Ph.D. in American History from Northern Illinois University and studied environmental chemistry at the University of Illinois at Chicago.

In addition to his academic work, he has long been active as a first-person historical interpreter, portraying figures such as Crispus Attucks; a Pilgrim at Plimoth Patuxet; an African American Civil War veteran; and a Wampanoag elder.

Throughout his career, Rice has been active in community and political organizing, including service with the Illinois Black Panther Party (1969–1974), the Southeast Side Environmental Task Force, and People for Community Recovery in Altgeld Gardens. He lives in Chicago with his family and continues to write stories and perform historical interpretations in Pembroke, Illinois.